I0568408

Arts Hustler
A Story of Resilience

By *OUR CLASS* producer Sofia Kapkov
In collaboration with Anastasia Chernikova

NEW YORK, 2025

Copyright © 2025 by MART Foundation
All rights reserved.

No part of this publication may be reproduced, distributed, or transmitted in any
form or by any means, including photocopying, recording, or other electronic or
mechanical methods, without the prior written permission of the publisher, ex-
cept as permitted by U.S. copyright law. For permission requests, contact MART
Foundation at info@martfdn.org

Book cover design by Gosha Chubukin
Author's photo on the cover by Kirill Simakov
Photos courtesy of MART Foundation
First edition: 2025

Paperback ISBN: 979-8-218-67053-5
eBook ISBN: 979-8-218-67054-2

To my kids Anastasia, Ivan, and Zoe.
You are my best projects, love you endlessly.

Praise for *Arts Hustler* and *Our Class*

Arts Hustler is is an extraordinary story of personal courage and reinvention. A Russian woman gives up a life of privilege in Moscow to protest the war in Ukraine, and through relentless effort, becomes a successful theatre producer in New York. A compelling and inspiring read."

— Alexander Rodnyansky,
Academy Award-Nominated Producer

"Sofia's inspiring journey is a true catharsis."

— Odessa Rae,
Academy Award-Winning Producer

"Sofia Kapkov is a force of nature. Leaving behind a highly successful producing career in Russia, she picked herself up and began again in the United States. With courage, determination, and skillful business acumen, she made an invaluable contribution to an off-Broadway play that became a huge success. Her story is a lesson for all who are summoning the courage to begin again."

— Annie Hamburger,
Executive Artistic Director, En Garde Arts

"This is a powerful book, especially for anyone starting in a new country. I've been there myself, so I really get what Sofia's talking about. Her honesty, her energy, the way she keeps moving forward no matter what — it's seriously inspiring."

— Ivan Vyrypaev, Playwright

"The audience delivered an impassioned ovation!"

— *The New Yorker* about *Our Class*

"The entire cast is excellent."

— *The Wall Street Journal* about *Our Class*

"Artistically ambitious."

— *The New York Times* about *Our Class*

Introduction

The first time I saw *Our Class* was in January 2024 at the BAM stage in New York. My friends had been buzzing about it, so I bought a ticket without expecting much. The room was packed with some familiar faces — for one, Chulpan Khamatova, the most well-known Russian actress, standing in line behind me. By the end of the play, everyone was crying and giving a standing ovation. I felt like I'd stumbled onto something rare, which doesn't happen often in New York, a city saturated with events that strive to present something special, so it's harder to be moved deeply.

A few months later, I met Sofia — a producer I'd first heard of back in Moscow when we both still lived there. She had opened the city's most important creative hub: a Documentary Film Center that united the creative class around the most progressive films. At the time, I was working in newsrooms as a reporter and editor, interviewing entrepreneurs and writing stories.

Now, Sofia invited me to meet in New York, where she had moved after the invasion of Ukraine in 2022.

She was confident, bold, always in motion; her energy contagious, though I didn't know what the deal was. She told me she'd been keeping a diary since moving to New York, thinking it might turn into a book, and that I could help write it. A few days later, I was already interviewing Sofia in a three-hour conversation.

So, a few words about the play itself: *Our Class* was written by Tadeusz Slobodzianek, a famous Polish playwright, who explored historical trauma; precisely, how personal relationships are shattered by nationalism and violence.

It's a terrifying story, based on real events that took place in Poland in 1941, during the pogrom in the town of Jedwabne, of ten classmates who grew up together. They were friends who loved playing games, dreaming about the future, and falling in love. Some of them were Catholic, some Jewish, though in the beginning, none of that mattered. Then history intervened. Poland was torn apart — first by Soviet occupation, then by the brutal German invasion. Tensions rose when neighbors turned against neighbors, and hatred, once hidden, began to grow. Betrayal became easier than loyalty. You watch this play and see how quickly people who once loved each other became enemies and how kindness could turn into cruelty, how a boy who once loved a girl could later rape her. The most horrifying moment comes when 1,600 Jewish men, women, and children are locked in a barn and burned alive by their own neighbors. And then the story asks: What happened to the classmates who witnessed this nightmare? How did they live the rest of their lives, carrying such memories, such guilt, such silence? What did they tell their children? What did they tell themselves in their final days? Did they ever dare to ask: What have I done? Could I have done something differently? *Our Class* isn't just the story of one town — it's an exploration of human nature. About how thin the line is between friendship and hatred, how ordinary people can be swept into horror, and how, long after the violence has ended, the questions never go away.

Our Class had a sold-out run at BAM in the winter of 2024 and received multiple Drama League award nominations, including "outstanding revival of a play." *The New York Times* called its artistic director, Igor Golyak, "one of the most inventive directors working in the United States," and *The New Yorker* pointed out the "impassioned ovation" for the show.

Sofia had just cut ties with her homeland, Russia, and moved to New York with three kids and two suitcases in February 2022, following the invasion of Ukraine, when this idea struck her. As she grieved the loss of her country, the family and friends she had left behind, she sought ways to heal. *Our Class* felt hauntingly relevant in a world that was growing increasingly divisive, where public discourse often devolved into sudden attacks of one kind or another.

In less than three years, Sofia transformed from a woman grieving the loss of her homeland to a producer of a compelling off-Broadway show. This book chronicles her transformation, taking readers behind the scenes of staging and living through a play in the theater capital of the world. Here, we see Sofia reshaped by the reality of a city where she is no one, after once standing at the peak of her career in Moscow.

We wrote this book for anyone caught in between — whether stuck in life or starting anew, redefining dreams and goals while clinging to hope. For immigrants who find themselves in New York, whether by choice or by chance, the book serves as a beacon of inspiration for new beginnings and a testament to resilience. "Whatever you do, there's going to be a good end. If it's not good enough yet, it means it's not the end," is a line Sofia likes to repeat and something I absorbed from her while working together.

— Anastasia Chernikova,
New York, February 2025

Prologue

One thing you need to know up front about being forced into immigration is that it's not going to be easy. In fact, nothing worthwhile ever comes easy, as everything in life comes at a cost. If you have principles and take a stand, sooner or later, you will face the consequences. For me, after Putin launched the war in Ukraine in 2022, the answer was clear: I had to cut ties with my homeland as I knew that I wanted no part in this chaos. The cost was leaving behind my comfortable life — my heartfelt projects, a lovely apartment, and, more importantly, my parents and friends.

Here in New York, I often draw strength from within, fueled by a belief that good intentions and the impact we leave in others' lives open doors for those who keep pushing forward. I find myself creating something far bigger than me — something so vital that giving up isn't an option.

Dreaming doesn't hurt either. In fact, it's my tool for survival. Research shows that people following their dreams and, subsequently, goals are more likely to endure. There is a book that seems to be on the shelf of every psychotherapist: Viktor Frankl's *Say Yes to Life*. Through real-life examples, Frankl illustrates how those who find meaning and purpose are best equipped to withstand and even thrive under the most harrowing circumstances. I'm not comparing my experiences to the unimaginable suffering endured by those in concentration camps. But I do believe that forced immigration, regardless of one's income or social status, is always a kind of rebirth. You can never be fully prepared for it; it always catches you off guard.

And yet, with tens of thousands of immigrants arriving in New York each year, the city is the melting pot of the world, a cauldron full of some of the most successful people who have risen as leaders in their newfound hometown. They didn't succeed despite the challenges they faced; they succeeded because of them. New York is a city that embraces failure, allowing us to fail, learn, and try again. It was the great Samuel Beckett who said we had to "fail better." That's perfect for me — someone who perceives life as a journey paved with stumbles and missteps.

When I first arrived in New York as a tourist many years ago, I was overwhelmed by its beauty, freedom, and opportunities. The Big Apple seemed like a dream. When I immigrated here, reality hit me hard. I felt stuck by what seemed like insurmountable obstacles, learning a new language, adapting to a new identity, and creating a new social circle. These difficulties led to frustration, yet also made me even more determined and ambitious. One challenge I had to overcome was my desire to turn things around fast. In this new, strange environment, I had to adjust my expectations surrounding the pace of my achievements. In fact, I was devastated when things didn't unfold as quickly as I'd hoped. For some time, I avoided meeting people who reminded me of how far behind I was, of how much ground I still had to cover.

It was a far cry from my life back in Moscow, where I was a well-known producer and arts hustler. I began working very early. When I had just turned seventeen I became a TV anchor for the most popular show for teenagers. Since then, I have produced major television shows, started the only documentary film theater in the country, launched the first non-fiction streaming platform, ran the largest contemporary ballet festival, and planned to open the first contemporary ballet company myself. Here in New York, though, I had to start from scratch at the age of forty-three. That didn't stop me from embarking on my first play as a theater producer. Here's a fun fact: Before coming to the Big Apple, I didn't even know the exact difference between off-Broadway and Broadway. But after two years of dedicated work, we managed to bring *Our Class* to a famous New York stage, the Brooklyn Academy of Music (BAM), in January 2024, and a year later received four major awards at the prestigious

Lucille Lortel Awards, including Best Ensemble and Best Revival.

I'm thrilled to say it became more than a job or a breakthrough project for me; it evolved into a life-changing experience. Since arriving in New York on February 27, 2022, I've found myself reflecting on the Ukraine War and the underlying causes of violence. I watched sixty-nine out of the seventy-nine performances of *Our Class*, crying each and every time. I wept not only because of the dramatic events that mirrored those in our play but because I was overwhelmed with sorrow for the people dying in this senseless war. I also cried for my own life, for all that I have lost. Those tears helped me heal. I always believed that true art was a form of healing, but this time I felt it in my very soul. This time the art that I produced healed me. My traumas became less pronounced as I began to push aside the barriers that had hindered me from enjoying my new life in my new city.

I wasn't alone in this healing process. Every member of our acting team admitted it was not merely another performance but a transformative experience, one that we all shared. And, believe me, I found that actors in New York are hard to surprise. We spent a lot of time discussing the play, posing questions to ourselves, wisdom that was then conveyed through the performances to our audiences. We didn't want to preach or teach a lesson, instead, we aimed to prompt introspection that would lead to finding answers within. I believe this is how the healing power of art can break through. Just as the most impactful works, like Akram Khan's ballet *Giselle*, the documentary *Act of Killing*, or books by Erich Maria Remarque, *Our Class* transformed life-changing, healing experiences through pain, tears, and introspection.

The hardships and challenges of producing the play became my greatest mentors. Based on real events, the play's tragic moments — brought to life so powerfully by our actors — stripped away the illusions of everyday life, revealing what truly matters and the price we're willing to pay for our actions and dreams. As a producer, my ultimate goal was to heal souls through art — and that journey began with healing my own.

I didn't want to create a play about something that bad people did in the past. First of all, I don't divide people into good and bad. I believe that we, as humans, can do good things, but unfortunately we can't avoid doing bad things. Like one of my favorite books, Dostoevsky's *Crime and Punishment*, shows, there are no inherently good or bad people; rather, there are actions for which we take responsibility for every minute of the day and night, and that is what shapes our lives.

So my goal was to pull this play out of the specific timeline of 1941 and make it timeless, something people from various backgrounds could relate to. And it happened — while watching the show, Jewish audiences see one thing, Russians and Ukrainians another, and Poles have a whole different perspective. What's more, I heard from Black Americans that the play resonated directly with their experiences and deeply touched a chord.

While working on the production of *Our Class*, I lost count of how many times I was told it couldn't be done. When a well-known Broadway producer whom I asked for advice said that I wouldn't be able to make it as a no-name producer with a tight budget, for a moment I actually considered letting it go. We were turned down by a venue that later welcomed us back, calling it the first show to earn daily standing ovations. There were countless other challenges, with some members even trying to convince me to cancel the opening night as they thought it wasn't worth pushing through. But when you have a dream, it's not just work anymore — it's something you live for. It becomes life itself. The road is hard, but for me it is one that I've been on since I was a kid. My family left our village of Lipovtsy — a tiny spot in the Far East of Russia with just four buildings, flatlands, and cornfields within a military garrison — for Moscow when I was thirteen years old. I remember my school teacher cautioning me, "You're going to Moscow, but reset your expectations — it will be hard to succeed there, you'll always be provincial for them." Then, years later, in the winter of 2022, the same arguments were being made in Russia as I prepared to leave for New York. People back in Moscow were quick to remind me that nobody was waiting for me there (which was true, of course, but hearing it from others didn't help).

I was lucky, in a sense, that I was prepared for struggle from an early age by not having the happiest childhood. My parents divorced, followed by a bloody battle for custody, while I wasn't able to see either of them and lived with my grandmother. Then, one day, my mother showed up with another man and said, "This is your father now." I was lucky; he happened to be a great person and he became my true dad.

Finding my own way and trusting my gut — which I rely on in most of my life experiences — has been with me for a while too. When I was six years old, I took a bus by myself to and from a music school in the neighboring village. One day after class, I found that the bus had broken down. Undaunted, I decided to walk. I ended up walking for five hours — through forests, villages, and so on. My mother nearly lost her mind, but I made it home.

Another time, I was eleven. One day, I stayed late at school because I was assigned to be on duty, cleaning the blackboard and running other chores. The bus didn't notice I wasn't there and left without me. I walked out of the school, not knowing what to do, and decided to walk home — ten or fifteen kilometers. It was a snowy, sunny day, probably about minus thirty degrees, a freezing Russian winter. I remember the bright sun and the bone-chilling cold. At one point, I thought I wouldn't make it, and I imagined how angry my mother would be, cursing that the snow would bury me and she would not be able to find my body until next spring. I made it almost to the settlement but lost consciousness on the way. But soldiers spotted me from their tower and came to get me.

I learned the hard way how to be a survivor, and even if I don't want my kids to ever have this experience, I know that I've learned a lot from it. Most importantly, how to trust yourself and tune out the noise, whether from the outside or within your own mind. It doesn't matter whether you come from Senegal, Mexico, Russia, or anywhere else — if you don't let fear hold you back, you can end up where you want, finding a way to do something you love, and maybe — just maybe — create something that makes a difference.

Still, I realize this is easier said than done. In this book, I will be talking about the specific qualities that one must nurture to get to where you want to go. People have often told me how brave I am for starting from scratch with three kids and half my life behind me. I always respond that it's resilience that helps me push through. This is something anyone can cultivate within themselves. Immigrants coming to America often feel hopeless and lost, just as I did. Yet many soon thrive and learn to enjoy their lives again.

In these turbulent times when so many people are displaced and forced to move between countries, I wanted to share my experiences of building a new life in a new country. You have to be creative, sometimes inventing your own rules, staying true to yourself but also trusting others, and relying on your beliefs — even when no one else does. It is challenging, but I hope this book will show that it is not a bad thing.

One more thing: I know that I'm not always easy to be around, especially since I don't take "no" for an answer. I also know what I want, and I do everything I can to achieve it. I'm not perfect, but I never claimed to be the angel. When I wrote this book, I aimed for complete honesty. The first draft was filled with personal memories and names, but after some thought, I decided to remove some names to respect people's privacy. Although there is no explicit political content in the book, my stance on the war is clear. I don't want my words to cause any trouble for those living in Moscow. I realize not everyone wants to be associated with me or this book, and that's something I need to respect.

And the last, If I had the chance to meet myself three years ago, the only advice I'd give would be this: "Please, if you fail, always remember that it's okay. It means you're growing — so just keep going." If I have any fervent wish, it is that newcomers will read this book and it inspires them to find the strength to keep going and to find a way to realize and live out their dreams.

Chapter 1

I've always trusted my intuition. So when in February 2022, I felt a weighty stone lodged in my chest, manifesting as a panic attack, I knew something was about to shift. During the prior ten months, I'd been working on a new project in Moscow, where I lived at that time: My team and I were building a new contemporary ballet company. Even in those fraught times, I believed in my reputation as an arts producer, someone who could bridge cultures with the West and, in this case, unite the best ballet dancers with the best choreographers in the world. In Russia, we had a great legacy of classical dance — everyone knew about the Bolshoi and Mariinsky theaters, but not as much had been achieved in contemporary dance. I wanted to change that. I convinced the world's best choreographers to come to Russia and create work for Russian dancers each season. We were supposed to announce the new company in March 2022.

Once, I was called "Dyagilev in skirt" as a joke, and I thought it would be ideal to announce our project on the 150th birthday of Sergei Diaghilev, the ballet impresario I admired. I thought cultural projects could exist apart from politics and make an impact on their own. In retrospect, I can see how stupid and naive I was for feeling that way.

I got that foreboding sensation three days before Russia attacked Ukraine on February 24, 2022, in what we now know as the largest war in Europe since World War II. In the days before the tanks rolled across the border, I asked my Ukrainian and American friends, people from my circle in London and Moscow, the same question: "Do you think Putin is crazy enough to do it?" Nobody knew the answer or was expecting such an escalation.

On the Wednesday evening before the invasion, my new friend from Washington, D.C., whom I met just a few months earlier when I was on vacation with my youngest daughter, Zoe, texted me, asking if I was in New York. At the time, I was traveling back and forth to visit my oldest daughter, Anastasia, who had gone to boarding school almost twelve years earlier, fallen in love with the States, decided to stay in New York after graduation from NYU in 2021, and had been living and working in the city.

I remember it so clearly, as if it were yesterday, what she told me after her first trip to California at the tender age of ten: "Mom, why do we live in Russia? I'm not going to live in this country. People aren't smiling here." What could I say? She wasn't wrong, my smart little girl.

I texted back to my friend in D.C. that fateful Wednesday, saying that I was in Moscow but scared as hell. He suggested I visit my daughter, and I took it as a sign, since I had been looking for answers. All night, I ran different scenarios through my mind: What if they close the border? What if I can't see my daughter again?

When I was a child, I had a nightmare: I was standing with a suitcase, unable to leave the country. I was in my forties at the time, so I remembered life in the Soviet Union very well, where you were not allowed to travel freely. For me, the idea of being stuck with two younger kids in Moscow while my eldest daughter was in New York was just too painful to bear.

The invasion began at dawn, and I hadn't slept that night, monitoring the news. I was thinking about my friends in Kharkiv, Ukraine. I texted them but didn't hear back. Only later did I find out that they had gone into hiding in their own basement and watched, through their security cameras, as Russian forces entered their village and looted empty houses. Since it was a gated community where most residents had surveillance systems, they were able to see intruders roaming through their properties. On the third day, the wife couldn't take it any longer, so she decided to leave while the husband chose to stay. She jumped in the car with her daughter, her elderly mother, and a few neighbors, and they headed for the border.

3

My friend told me everything two years later, when we finally saw each other in Turkey. She described how, in just one day, her successful life collapsed — going from being a wealthy entrepreneur and protected wife living in a beautiful home to a new reality where she had to witness corpses on the road, sleep in the car for days without a shower, and live with the fear of not knowing if she'd wake up the next morning. She's okay now, still beautiful and brave, but divorced and living in a foreign country, building a new life by baking cakes and selling cooking classes on Instagram. Fun fact: She was the one who insisted we send our ten-year-old daughters to summer camp in California.

That morning on Thursday, February 24, 2022, I learned that all my plans were ruined. Of course, I cared about the people in Ukraine, who didn't? But it was hard not to be selfish about my circumstances. My life was about to be turned upside down. I had put so much effort into this contemporary dance project, I'd worked so hard, and I wanted it so badly. And now what? That's it? Because someone in charge decided he wanted war more than we wanted life? What the fuck? Our ballet company wasn't going to happen. I kept watching the news, sobbing. Then I called my ex-husband and told him I made a decision to fly to New York and was taking our four-year-old daughter with me. It was winter break at the American school Zoe attended in Moscow. For the first time in her life, she was spending the holidays with her dad, who took her to Dubai. A lot of Russians like that place — not really my thing — but it was warm, and Zoe was happy there. They were supposed to stay one more day, and I told them there was no need to change their tickets, that we would leave the day after their arrival. Zoe's dad said I was overreacting and that we would talk about it when he got back. I didn't want to wait, so I booked us tickets to New York right away.

My next move was to run quickly to the nearest attorney's office that I usually used for legal matters. There, I signed all the necessary documents, giving my assistant and my parents the authority to act on my behalf if needed. Essentially, I authorized them to sell my apartment, close all my bank accounts, and disconnect my Russian phone number. I didn't give myself the chance to sit and think about it; rather, I just did what I thought was necessary.

The next day, Zoe returned from vacation. She looked radiant — beautiful, happy, and suntanned — while her dad seemed irritated. We ended up getting into a fight. It was bad. Not because we had never fought before — we're regular people, and people fight — but under those circumstances, it felt even more dramatic.

I've been married twice and, as I used to say, "happily divorced" twice. My first relationship lasted thirteen years. We were young students, stupid kids, when we married. We behaved even more recklessly when we divorced, although I was already an established producer, he was a famous politician, and we had two kids together. Long story short, we didn't manage to remain close friends.

My second marriage was shorter, but we started our romantic journey as mature adults. I always admired my second husband. At some point, he felt like a hero not only to me but to many people in Moscow whom we called the creative class. Even when we failed as a couple, we remained friends because we shared common values, or so I thought.

I was confident that he would understand me and support my decision, but he didn't. He said, "What are you doing? Where are you going? Are you out of your mind? Stop acting like an idiot; it's not the last plane from Moscow to New York!" He slammed the door shut on me and left without saying goodbye.

In a few hours, I began receiving calls from partners, venues, choreographers, and artists canceling their plans, saying they couldn't be involved anymore. They didn't have to explain, but a few felt so bad they served their bitter pill with honey, saying that they loved me and respected me and that they were confident we would work together again in the future.

It was a disaster. I had a meeting with my team. I'd been working in Moscow all my life. My team was almost thirty people. At that time, I had a streaming platform for documentary films and was a successful movie theater for documentary and art lovers that had shown fifteen thousand films in almost ten years of existence. I was also a founder of a Russian non-profit organization that helped artists in Russia and an American nonprofit organization that was responsible for touring and collaboration with foreign artists. This meant my team was busy, especially during that period of time when we were working on a new ambitious project. I'd heard many times that people liked to work with me; I was known as someone who was tough but fair, very passionate, but not one to cross the line. I cried when I watched ballet, but this was the first time I cried in front of my team, sobbing like a baby, exhibiting unprofessional and stupid behavior.

They had never seen me like this before. I announced that all projects were put on hold. The Seasons — the name of the new ballet company — was not going to happen. I managed to arrange an agreement with our donor, who allowed us to use his investment from our never-going-to-happen ballet company to help people make ends meet for a while. He had always been the most generous and thoughtful, cultural businessman with strong empathy, and working with him was a blessing. Thanks to his generosity, we were able to pay salaries up front for the next few months. During that meeting with my team, I said that everyone should decide on what was the best for them and their families. In my case, I was blunt: I said, "I am leaving. I don't know for how long. For the first time in my entire life, I don't have any plans."

It was a shock for everyone, of course, and as I understand now, announcing it that way to them was too much for some people who were not ready for such a conversation. Some decided to leave, some left and came back, and as of now, only three people from my former team are working for me.

But this is a thing about me: I make decisions fast. I am a speed demon; I can't even walk slowly. Once I have a feeling, I need to move quickly.

The day before, I called my mom and told her about my decision. I was surprised by how easily she took it. She said she would come help me pack and that my family supported me. I was caught off-guard because my relationship with my mom had always been rocky. I quite often felt like an unloved daughter and not the son they wanted instead. I couldn't help myself but think that I was never good enough for them. Maybe it wasn't them. Maybe it was the demons inside me that made me feel that way. Regardless, my mom, my dad, and my sister came over to help me pack while I sobbed.

They witnessed my fight with Zoe's dad, my unprofessional Zoom with my coworkers, and stood by me while I was packing. When my close friend called to check on me, I almost screamed: "It's all like a nightmare. I don't know what to do, or even what to pack! Nothing fits in two suitcases!"

"Calm down," she said. "Just pack one pair of jeans, one pair of heels, one dress, two sweaters. It's cold in New York. Don't forget to bring all the documents! The rest you'll figure out later."

When I had to tell my mom that I had no more plans and wouldn't be able to help her financially anymore, it was incredibly hard to say out loud. My mom had cancer, and I'd spent the last ten years doing everything I possibly could to support her. There were regular treatments in Moscow, trial treatments in Israel, and expensive care in Arkansas and New York. It helped her — despite the doctors' initial prediction of only a few months left to live — and she was able to live a fulfilling life. I love my mom — she's a tough cookie. I think my own resilience comes from my maternal family line. My grandmother and my mom shaped me into who I am today.

Later that day, I went to say goodbye to my best friend, who lived nearby. She was sophisticated, smart, always stayed calm, and she helped me become a better version of myself. We spent the entire Covid-19 lockdown together, and during that time, she wasn't just a camp friend — she was my therapist and trainer. Thanks to her superpower, I, a person who had always hated sports, started running. When I finally saw my mom after the lockdown, she said, "It looks like you have the best relationships in your life; you look so happy." And my mom was right. My friend helped me stay calm and sane. So now, looking back, I realize that if she had tried to stop me from leaving, I might have reconsidered. I knew she would stay behind. It would be difficult for us to stay as close with an ocean between us, but she supported my decision. We drank white wine, talked about everything, hugged, and then I left. On my way home — just a few blocks away — I was sobbing. I didn't know when I'd be able to see her again.

The next morning, I left behind my comfortable life in a beautiful Moscow apartment, along with the dreams and the career I had spent so long building as a successful arts producer. But above all, I made my children leave their lives behind. My daughter, Zoe, was only four years old, and my son, Ivan, was fifteen. I told them we were flying to see their sister in New York. Zoe was happy — she loved traveling and missed her sister, Anastasia. Ivan, however, wasn't happy at all. I remember him repeatedly asking, "But it's just for a week, right?" And all I could say was, "We'll see…"

At the airport, there was no sense of panic — it felt like an ordinary day. The only difference was that the customs officers asked my son and me more questions than usual about his father, who was a Russian opposition politician and former State Duma member. Known for his vocal criticism of Vladimir Putin, Dmitry was expelled from the Duma in 2016. In 2021, he fled to Ukraine, citing political persecution. In 2024, a Russian court sentenced him in absentia to eight years in prison for spreading "false information" about the Russian military. He was already living abroad, but his outspoken opposition to Putin had made him a well-known figure. Fun fact: My whole life, I'd strived to avoid politics, seeing it as a dirty, manipulative game, but somehow I'd been married to two politicians.

I'd always hated standing in line for boarding, so we sat near the gate. I noticed that most of the passengers were American residents. They spoke Russian but carried American documents. It seemed like many were leaving. I had already received a few emails suggesting it was time to go — one from the private American school my daughter attended in Moscow and another from a club called American Women in Moscow where I had once been a speaker, sharing my experience as a successful Moscow arts hustler.

My kids and I boarded a Russian Aeroflot plane. Back then, I could afford business class tickets for long-distance flights, so I had champagne, and my kids were busy using WiFi. Passing through Europe en route to the U.S. passengers kept checking their phones, watching in real time as more countries closed their airspace to Russian planes. It almost felt like a strangely entertaining game, and we considered ourselves lucky as the situation escalated. One by one, countries shut their skies, but we managed to slip through Europe just in time.

After more than one-third of the way, seven hours in the air, when we were about to enter Canada, the captain made an announcement — "Dear passengers, we have unpleasant news for you. The authorities in Canada have closed their airspace for all Russian aircrafts." The pilot added that it was the first such incident not only in his career but in the history of international aviation.

The WiFi was shut down immediately. Panic erupted; people were yelling and crying, and some were in need of medical assistance. Russian news immediately reported what the unhuman West did. Zoe's dad would later admit that he was wrong: Our plane was indeed the last direct flight from Moscow to New York.

However, we didn't get to New York as planned. We hung in the air for an indefinite time before they found a solution: to send us back to Sheremetyevo Airport in Moscow. My youngest daughter was okay, but my son wasn't. Ivan was on the spectrum. We were kicked out of eight different schools, and teachers always called him a piece of work. He didn't want to leave in the first place and had a tough time handling emotions. On top of it, a woman next to us on the plane was screaming, repeating the word "war" over and over, so my daughter Zoe started nagging me for an answer — what does "war" mean? I gulped down a glass of champagne that I had on my table since departure. The airplane directive, "You should put your own oxygen mask on first before helping others," kept running through my mind. That quote and that glass of champagne helped to ease my breathing and calm me down to start to explain to my four-year-old daughter what the word "war" meant. It wasn't easy. You have to be honest with kids, otherwise they sense the lie. But I didn't want to go into all the details because I didn't want to scare her even more: we had our family back in Russia. When I finished, she nodded, put her earphones with cute bunny ears back on, and continued watching *Masha and the Bear*, a beloved cartoon in Russia made for kids. When I boarded that plane, I didn't know how long I would be gone, but after explaining the meaning of war to my daughter, I knew I was never going back.

Emotionally, it was like descending into a mine. I still didn't know what to expect from my new life, but at that time, thirty thousand feet in the air, I realized it was a turning point with a one-way ticket.

Later, some people would call me a betrayer, but back then I felt that I was betrayed by my home country. And what was I expecting? I was born in a small town in Siberia, and two generations of my ancestors had been exiled there. We had no assets, no businesses that relatives could pass on to their children like almost any family in the history of Russia, thanks to wars, communism, censorship, and dekulakization.

I smirked as I remembered how, just two months earlier, for my birthday in December, my colleagues had given me memoirs of Russian ballet dancers who had emigrated in the early nineteenth century. The most striking were Vera Krasovskaya's *Nijinsky*, the famous memoirs of Matilda Kshesinskaya, and a lesser-known book by Nina Tikhonova, *The Girl in Blue*, which left a surprisingly deep impression on me.

How fitting, I thought. They once had it all but lost everything in a single day like me. They mopped floors, worked with high-pressure washers, sold clothes, and opened ballet schools. What if this was my future? In short, those books had mentally prepared me for this sudden immigration. I was so moved by their stories that only a few months after arriving in the United States, I was even considering opening a ballet school in New York. If you think that I opened it eventually, you are mistaken. My path was different, but let's go back.

We were flying back to Moscow. I didn't know what to do, so I was panicking. Once the WiFi started working, I received a lot of texts from my friends. One of them even bought me new tickets — from Moscow to Istanbul — so that my kids and I would be free to go to New York from Turkey.

I'm incredibly grateful for all my friends. Sometimes, I feel like I don't deserve their kindness. I get so caught up in my life and my art projects that I forget birthdays, or miss simple things like sending flowers to say thank you for their support and love. I often wonder — what is friendship, really? Is it about loyalty, convenience, shared values, or just familiar habits? Why do some people keep the same friends for a lifetime, while others seem to find new ones with each new chapter of their lives? I don't have a friend I've been close with since I was a kid. Maybe it's because we changed many locations and schools or maybe it's because I am too difficult to deal with, and that only makes me more grateful for the people who choose to stick around and accept me as I am. Friends mean the world to me, I don't know how I could have made it through without them.

We waited for a few hours before boarding the flight to Istanbul. At that time, I didn't feel anything:

I was just following the steps mechanically from one terminal to another. There were no issues at the border in Istanbul, and we took the next flight to New York. On this second plane, a woman overheard me speaking to my son and asked me in Russian where we resided. I really didn't know what to say; besides, I was too exhausted to come up with an answer. I said I didn't know and added that we were from Moscow. She then took pity on us — oh, you are refugees! The phrase unsettled me: I was successful, still wearing nice clothes and carrying an expensive bag — not the image of a refugee I had in my head. And yet, here I was — accepting my newly minted identity for the first time.

I didn't know how to respond. I wasn't technically a refugee. I already had my American documents. In 2016, I flew to New York to visit my eldest daughter while pregnant with my third child. One day in November, I fainted on the street. My doctor advised me not to fly, so I stayed in New York. It was a beautiful golden fall. I'd never liked autumn in gray and sad Moscow, but in New York, every season was so pretty. I didn't have much to do besides reading, and one day while browsing online, I found out it was the last day to apply for a diversity visa, or green card, as people usually call it. I googled the rules, filled out the forms online, and then promptly forgot about it. In April, I gave birth to my angel Zoe. A few weeks later, I found out that I'd earned a green card. New York brought me luck.

I want to pause here for a second. Some might say, "Oh, of course, she could leave — she was just a privileged bitch with a green card."

Let me be clear: I would have left even if I hadn't had it. Sure, maybe I couldn't have done it in three days. Maybe I would have had to figure out a tourist visa first. But if I had that tourist visa, I would have done the same. If you're an artist or work in the creative industry and you speak English, the U.S. actually makes the immigration process pretty manageable. I'm not saying it's easy, but you can enter on a tourist visa, change your status to a talent-based visa while you're already here, and eventually apply for a green card. That's what I would have done. Not having a green card wouldn't have stopped me. I didn't leave because I had a green card. I left because I didn't want to stay in a country where raising my kids would mean teaching them that living through a war is normal. I didn't want to accept the war. I didn't want to legitimize it. It was my choice.

So in 2017, when I was lucky to acquire a green card, I considered it a sign and shortly thereafter registered my first American company, MART Foundation, a nonprofit dedicated to producing and supporting contemporary performing arts programs with the goal of promoting independent Russian artists in the United States. In those prewar days, it was reasonable to believe as I did that we were entering a new global era, where everyone was open and eager to support each other. Since then, I've been involved in creating and supporting arts projects both in Russia and abroad. It was always a dream of mine to move to New York one day, but it was never the right moment. My mom was sick, and I knew I wouldn't be able to take her to the States. Zoe's dad lived in Moscow, and she was too little to be separated from him, so I guess the war made this move for me.

Anyway, after another ten hours on a plane, we finally landed at JFK in New York. My friend allowed us to stay in his apartment until I figured things out. I had asked him for a week, but how naive I was — I ended up staying for a month.

Soon after arriving in New York, sanctions hit all Russian banks, and all my cards stopped working. I borrowed some money and began to figure it all out. Every morning I called my mom. She helped me by keeping Zoe occupied while I was cooking or running errands by reading her Russian books on FaceTime. Every afternoon, I took Zoe to a playground, and she was an angel as usual. Her brother locked himself in his room and barely talked to me. It was a very cold March in New York that year, and every day I prayed that the war would end soon.

Chapter 2

Before the war in Russia, I was living a rich social life, attending premieres of the latest plays and ballets a few times a week. In 2013, I created the only Documentary Film Center in the country and every week had hosted premieres of movies shown at the center. Now, nine years later in New York, I had nothing to do and nowhere to go.

I clearly remember one episode. Overwhelmed, I'd been holed up at my friend's beautiful apartment for days, feeling that I overstayed my welcome. Then I got an invitation to a party in Manhattan. I didn't ask the host any questions; at that time of my life, moments when I didn't have to make decisions were rare, and I was grateful that someone else was taking the lead.

I didn't even have a proper outfit. I still didn't receive my stuff from Moscow, my parents just agreed to pack my clothes and send it to New York. My friend told me not to worry. She insisted on helping me with makeup and lent me a stunning dress with a chic purse. I asked Ivan to babysit his sister and went out.

It was a warm spring night when I arrived at the gathering. I was impressed by the magnificent interior adorned with beautiful flowers and an eclectic mix of fascinating guests.

The host and his girlfriend mingled with famous friends, one of them was Francis Ford Coppola. When I walked in and saw him, panic washed over me. I met his daughter a few times — I'd attended Sofia's Coppola premiere of *The Bling Ring* in 2013 at The Cannes Film Festival, but I'd never met Francis Ford Coppola. I admired him deeply; he was like God to me.

I'd rubbed elbows with countless celebrities and big stars in a different prewar life. Thanks to the kindness of my many friends, I have fond memories of dancing with Leonardo DiCaprio, chatting with Nicole Kidman, partying with Mick Jagger, and even taking spin classes with Sting.

I'm not trying to impress you but rather to set the scene. This time felt different, though. How you feel about yourself is crucial, and in 2022 I felt like absolute shit. At one point, the hosts' girlfriend introduced me to Francis: "Please meet our friend Sofia; she left Russia because of the war — she's like a refugee now."

I don't remember the exact order of words, but you get the vibe. She was a kind person and said it in a very polite way, yet I almost fainted. It was utterly embarrassing. I was seated at a beautiful table, and beyond that, all I can recall is the overwhelming feeling of being small and miserable. The one line from my favorite song, Radiohead's *Creep*, kept running through my head: "I don't belong here." But then I wondered, where do I belong?

When guests got around to discussing the tense relations between Russia and the West, Francis posed questions to me. I felt a second wave of shame, this time about my struggles to speak proper English.

The film legend spoke passionately about his craft, especially, when he talked about the biggest project of his life: an upcoming movie for which he was willing to risk everything, including selling his winery, to make it happen.

I just sat there, staring and filled with admiration. The thought that this might have been a huge opportunity for me to document this incredible evening didn't even cross my mind. Normally, I wasn't shy about asking people for a photo, even if they said no — after all, you weren't going to die. But that night, I remained frozen. It felt like watching one of those absurd films where everything looks so pretty on the outside and darkness is hidden within.

It happened to be a celebration of Francis's birthday. I'm grateful to have this memory now, but at that time, I didn't feel so lucky. In fact, in the days after the party, I began sinking further into darkness. I barely went out. I didn't want to be introduced as a refugee again, but I also didn't have anything noteworthy to share. No one could say, as it used to be in Moscow, "Hey, meet Sofia: She's a great theater and dance producer, she is a hustler!"

Back in Russia, even after Crimea was annexed, many of us pretended that nothing happened and we had a good life. I was in shock when it happened, but I didn't do anything or even speak up about it. I thought that simply choosing never to go there would be enough. Some people from my crowd even made fun of me when this topic came up in conversations. "Oh... you should reconsider planning your birthday in Crimea; if you want Sofia to come, she is not gonna come, she is too stubborn." People laughed and I didn't say a word. I didn't stop being friends with people who saw the situation differently; I kept going to their premieres, restaurants, or gallery openings and numerous parties.

My Documentary Film Center was similar to the well-known one in New York, the IFC Center. We had many supporters, and we were blooming. Some people still believe my accomplishment was only due to my successful husband. It's easier for some to think a woman can't succeed without a man behind her — believing she can't be both smart and successful on her own. The truth is, of course, he helped me a lot — advocating for me, introducing me to many powerful people — and I am grateful for that. But I believe it wasn't because he fell for my green eyes. He did it because I was a creative, hardworking producer. In the end, the project was successful because I worked hard, not because I was fluttering my eyelashes.

In 2012, I was helping with the launch of a series at news agency RIA Novosti, where we screened and discussed documentaries every week. The initiative was well received, so I suggested expanding it into a full-fledged institution with daily screenings. The Moscow government agreed to support RIA with this project, and I spent a lot of time searching for a venue, ultimately finding a space at the Museum of Moscow, which was located next to RIA Novosti at the time. The agency was then led by a visionary executive. Together, we transformed an abandoned hangar into a modern cinema space, which later became the Documentary Film Center. Unfortunately, she was fired in 2013 due to the restructuring of RIA Novosti as part of a government initiative to control state-run media. But before she left, she told me that as DFC was my dream and I should find donors, take the project, and run it independently. And so I did.

I built an amazing team and started traveling to international festivals, trying to convince distributors to sell me films for 50 percent of their future royalties — we simply couldn't afford to pay full price. No one agreed at first, but eventually, I made some deals. Step by step, people began saying yes to my unusual proposal, and somehow, I even negotiated for the entire collection of Brett Ratner's films. Ratner was an American director and producer known for blockbusters like *Rush Hour* and *X-Men: The Last Stand*. He also produced numerous documentaries, including incredible *Night Will Fall* — a powerful film which showed gruesome scenes from newly liberated Nazi concentration camps. This all happened before his career was marred by allegations of sexual misconduct, but I've heard that he is working on a new documentary about Melania Trump, so I guess he is back in the game. When I met him, he was nice to me, and I told him that Russia had huge potential and that, in the future, he'd make good money.

Another big success for me was securing the rights to a new documentary about the singer and musician Amy Winehouse. I'd always admired her, and it was important for me to distribute the documentary in Russia. I remember going to the Cannes office of the company selling the rights. It was crowded with people, but I sat down and told them I wouldn't leave without finalizing the deal. After a few hours, I walked away with the contract, even though there were bigger producers interested. That was how I'd always operated — through persuasion.

In fact, persuasion made all the difference for me when I was just starting out. While studying journalism in Moscow, I worked as a producer at various TV channels. When I was just twenty-three years old, I found out that my professor knew the chief editor of *Namedni* — the most successful and respected news show at the time. I asked to be introduced to this important man. I then arranged a job interview with the editor for noon on a Monday. He didn't show up, so I waited and texted him. I kept waiting at the TV station for six hours before he finally replied to my text. When I wrote that I was still there, he responded: "Are you crazy? Go home!"

"Can I come back tomorrow?" I replied. He agreed. Looking back now, as an adult, I realize most people would have taken his absence as a sign and just left the station.

The next day, I showed up in anything but the typical reporter outfit. I was wearing high heels, a tiger-print skirt, and my long, curly hair was barely hiding large golden hoop earrings. I liked to rock this sleek, fashionable vibe. When I met the editor, I sensed his disdain for my outrageous look. He told me that two hundred people had already applied for the position and there was no chance he'd hire me without experience. Then I said: "Test me. You have nothing to lose. Give me an assignment." It was a producer role, and just to get rid of me, he agreed and told me to find out some information. I came back twenty minutes later with an exclusive interview arranged. He was in shock when I told him, "You can record the interview at this time tomorrow." That's how we ended up working together until Putin shut us down for our criticism, once comparing him to Gollum from *Lord of the Rings*.

Later, when I was about twenty-six or twenty-seven, I really wanted to be the editor-in-chief of the evening news. I told my boss I wanted the job, and she said she would never offer it to me because I was a woman. The irony was that she was a woman herself. So I moved to another channel where they did offer me the role.

In 2012, during Putin's election, censorship became unbearable — we were receiving calls from the Kremlin, demanding that we lie on air by changing the numbers in the election. That was when I quit, marking the end of my TV career.

That was a decade ago, so it gives you a sense of my fighting spirit, or, more accurately to say, my running spirit — because I'm not really a fighter; I'm more of a runner. When something stops working for me, I can't help it: I have to leave. That's why I always tell my daughter that while I love weddings, I might love divorce even more — if a relationship isn't working, it's always better to have a terrible ending sooner than to endure a never-ending.

So after seventeen years of working on TV, in 2012, I left without hesitation. Ten years later after, the full-scale invasion, I did the same when I took a stand against the war and moved to the U.S.

I canceled or postponed all projects with Russians, and as we immersed ourselves in new cultural communities, my team shifted our focus to supporting artists in the U.S., Europe, and Israel. We also stopped accepting any donations from Russia.

Chapter 3

One project I had hoped we would be involved in was a play directed by Dmitry Krymov, one of the most innovative theater directors in the world. He had been splitting his time between the U.S. and Russia like many others before the war broke out. At that time, he was directing an adaptation of Chekhov's final play, *The Cherry Orchard*, at the Wilma Theater in Philadelphia. As he was working on the project, with the premiere scheduled for April, someone from the production's team reached out to me a few months beforehand, explaining they were short on funds. The project sounded brilliant to me; besides, I'd always admired his talent. He had a remarkable ability to weave narratives into a unique visual design. The production team asked MART to partner with the theater, and we planned to take the production from Philly to New York after the premiere. I agreed and began fundraising for the project in the United States. Back in December 2021, I had managed to raise additional funds from the American donor for this project.

Two weeks before the premiere, we received an anonymous letter claiming my company was working with a Russian oligarch who financed the war. It was total bullshit, so I didn't take it seriously. The next day, a friend of mine, the artistic director of a prestigious New York venue, called me and said, "Sofia, I don't want to freak you out, but we received an anonymous email warning about partnering with MART because it allegedly works with Russian oligarchs who financed the war. I know it's not true, but I thought you should know."

The same email had been sent to several other partners, including the Wilma Theater. Under U.S. law, you can check all the funds that nonprofit organizations receive. MART accepted donations from Russians, just like many other European and American organizations, but the last donation was made before the war. What's more, MART never took money from the Russian government or from anyone who was advocating for the war. So it was a blatant lie. No one responded to this anonymous letter, but for some reason, the Wilma Theater, an organization that had never worked with me before, decided to make a public statement. They didn't discuss it with me and made a huge mistake in their announcement.

They falsely claimed that MART had given them money from a Russian oligarch. As a result, they decided to cease the partnership and return the donation. To make matters worse, they named the wrong person as their donor. It all felt so unfair. When they needed funds, they didn't care to ask who their donor was, but faced with this anonymous letter, they decided to make a statement to save face and throw me under the bus. As soon as we received the money, we sent it to support artists in Ukraine, as per our mutual decision with an American donor who was born in Ukraine. I resolved never to work with the Wilma Theater again. For the next few weeks, journalists tried to ruin my life, but eventually, they lost interest. Life went on. Still, I'm glad Krymov managed to stage his play, but I didn't go to see the show.

I was angry with the people who were trying to ruin my career here. Who on earth, living in the U.S. and doing their own thing, would send anonymous emails about a woman who had just moved to a new country? Clearly, I could have taken a different path and found success in Russia, like many still do. But here I was, exhausted from juggling my new life in America with three kids while trying to come up with new projects. I understand that we humans are not perfect and we quite often take advantage in situations like this. Maybe they were just considering me a new competitor in the market. Someone even told me that it could be Ukrainians. But I didn't want to speculate about it because I didn't have any proof. I believed in many things — intuition, signs, and also karma. So good luck to that person. But at the same time, I couldn't help but think that something I did in the past had come back to me this way.

Needless to say, this occurred during a challenging time. Tensions were rising not only between Ukrainians and Russians and between the West and Russia, but also among Russians themselves. In my case, I was falsely accused by people I know of receiving a pension from "Gosdep" (the term Russians used for the U.S. State Department). It wasn't true. Even those Russians who opposed the war began blaming each other: Emigrants were deemed traitors for abandoning the country and refusing to fight the regime, while those who stayed were criticized for continuing to pay taxes that funded the war. On top of it all, I was burning with shame, blaming myself. Like many who had lived in Russia, I questioned why I hadn't seen the invasion coming and what role I might have unconsciously played in it.

Chapter 4

By nature, I was a dreamer who always needed to create. Once I had something on my mind, I couldn't let it go. Besides, immersing myself in work proved to be the best medicine against "doomscrolling" and falling into a mental abyss. I wanted to take on new projects, but first I had to manage the mundane side of this life-changing situation.

Getting my kids into school was part of that. I looked into the best public schools since I couldn't afford the private ones anymore. One of the best schools in the city was the renowned PS 6, which, among others, J.D. Salinger and Lenny Kravitz had attended. I thought it would be a great start for my daughter, Zoe. My son ended up in a non-prestigious public high school on the Upper West Side, where he was the only white kid in his class.

I checked available apartments for rent on the Upper East Side, the neighborhood where PS 6 was located. In New York City, you could only send your child to the elementary school assigned to your ZIP code. There was just one place available in that area: tiny, ugly, and ridiculously expensive. I had to sign the lease right away because it was spring break, and my daughter needed to start school immediately afterward.

When I arrived at the open house that April morning, I was the first potential tenant. I stepped into the creepy one-bedroom apartment overlooking a narrow terrace that faced a wall, where I was to live for at least a year with my four-year-old daughter and fifteen-year-old son while trying to forget my beautiful five-bedroom apartment in the center of Moscow. I took a deep breath and said, "I'll take it." The realtor looked surprised, even more than I was, but he took the deposit and signed the contract. It wasn't worth it; it was more than I could afford, but I did it for my kids. We would have our place to live and Zoe would be off to the school of my choice the next Monday. Meanwhile, my son Ivan was grappling with some social issues. Diversity wasn't something we encountered much in Russia, so he found that change a challenge to overcome. Yet, two years later he graduated, which was a huge achievement. Navigating the health and educational departments felt like an uphill battle for me. Amid all the chaos, we had managed to find our footing.

Zoe's school life was truly a blessing. I'll never forget her first day at PS 6. When we arrived at the school yard, it was already crowded with people. I was even more nervous than Zoe — she was a brave little cookie. The day before, I had emailed her teacher to let her know we were coming, and the school principal had promised to give Zoe a quick tour after drop-off. When we found her class, there was already a line of kids with their parents standing behind them. As we approached, a beautiful woman with long blonde hair walked up to me and said in English, "Good morning. I assume you're Sofia? You're the new Russian family."

"Yes," I replied.

She said, "I want to introduce myself. My name is Tanya. I'm Ukrainian. My brother is still in Kyiv." I blushed and froze for a second. I didn't know what to expect — for a moment, I thought she might punch me, or who knows what. My hands trembled. It was all just a flash, but a thousand thoughts raced through my mind. Then she continued, "This is my daughter, Alina. We would love to invite Zoe over today for her very first play date. Play dates are a big part of school life here, and because of the war, I believe it's even more important that our children become friends." Tears welled up in my eyes. I whispered, "Thank you." From that moment, we switched to Russian — Tanya spoke it fluently. And yes, Zoe's first play date was with Alina. To this day, Alina is still Zoe's best friend. Of course, now they both speak only English and refuse to use Russian, but I'm just happy that we gave them the chance to build such a beautiful friendship, and I'm grateful to Tanya for that memory.

While my kids were in school, I focused on the future, spending most of my time in the small, spartan apartment. I could survive on my savings for a while, but I needed to act quickly, and I needed to find a job. In the meantime, in Moscow, my team was quitting, moving on to work for other institutions or simply using the brand that I built for their own benefit. I was happy for them, but I couldn't help feeling sad about myself.

One day in May, I was invited to see a non-verbal play called *Andre and Dorine* from Spain's Kulunka Teatro. Its review stated something like, "If there is a show that has more to say than this one about what it means to be human, I'd be surprised," and I was sold. But nothing prepared me for what I was about to witness.

Three incredible Spanish actors conveyed the poignant story of an elderly couple and their adult son without uttering a single word. They spoke through movement, puppetry, and masks, honoring the lives of two artists in love — a writer and a cellist — as they navigated the labyrinth of Alzheimer's as it slowly encroached on their minds and relationship. It was one of the best shows I'd ever seen, and believe me, I've experienced my fair share of theater productions.

The performance wasn't just emotional and charming; it was pure, profound art. By the end, I found myself in tears. But I wasn't alone: Everyone was crying, not just me. After the show, my friend asked me in a polite American way if I was okay and suggested I should talk to someone. The next day, she connected me with a psychologist from London who agreed to have a session with me pro bono. At first, I found it a bit odd, but then I realized she was trying to help, so why not give it a try? And, wow, what a gift that session was for me. That one-hour Zoom helped to change my perspective on reality.

The psychologist asked me a few questions, and we talked like old friends. My English was still shaky in those days, so I wasn't comfortable speaking with strangers. Yet, he gave me a comforting look and the feeling that he genuinely cared and understood what I was going through. I forgot about my English, my accent, and even about time. I had so much to share — I hadn't realized how much pain, anger, and unspoken thoughts I was harboring. I was exhausted from feeling lost, and I wanted to tell him everything. But he gently stopped me. "Sofia," he said, "I'm more than happy to hear your whole story, but I think I already get the idea. You are brilliant, bright, strong, and resilient, yet confused and tired. This is a challenging time for you. If you don't mind, I'd like to share a few ideas from my experience working with refugees and people with PTSD. First of all, we are all different, and we need to understand that significant changes in life can take one to three years to settle; people need this time to heal after dramatic events like these," he said. Then he continued: "Some people are able to recover from traumatic events within a year, while others may need three years or more — even if their experiences were seemingly less severe. We often judge ourselves harshly, but it's important to remember that healing doesn't follow a set timeline. Our bodies and neurological systems are built differently. Keeping this in mind, it's crucial not to be hard on yourself. Give yourself the time and patience you need to heal.

"Second, you can't rush things. I can see you have this amazing skill to make quick decisions, but now you need to slow down. Imagine you're like a horse who always wins the race, but one night, this horse wakes up in a dark forest. If the horse wakes up and gallops, she will probably die; the smart horse will pause, listen to the new sounds and smells, and slowly begin to wake up."

I almost screamed in response, then blurted out: "Oh, my God, that means I'm not the old horse; I'm just smart!"

"Exactly," he laughed.

In hindsight, this advice surrounding post-traumatic stress disorder seems simple and obvious, but at the time, it truly helped me. This gifted psychologist had given me official permission to slow down and stop stressing about why I wasn't doing anything. I began to use my time to contemplate what I actually wanted to do.

Chapter 5

I knew from the start that working with Russia was off the table, and I was beginning to sense that things weren't exactly falling into place in the U.S. either. Yet I still had a strong connection to Israel. I fell in love with Israeli dance during my tenure as CEO of the largest Russian contemporary dance festival called Context, which was founded by the ballet dancer Diana Vishneva. I collaborated with many Israeli dancers and toured Russian companies to Tel Aviv. In 2020, I was executive producer of the new festival MART based on Israel celebrating Russian culture and touring Russian theater companies there. I've never worked at any theater in Moscow, but I worked with the biggest Russian theater companies as a touring producer. After the war began, several members of my team had moved to Israel, so I was familiar with the market. I still had been working closely with a few Israeli choreographers, including the renowned Sharon Eyal. So my next idea seemed like a natural step: to create a special program that would foster collaboration between Israeli and American artists. I brainstormed some concepts and successfully fundraised. Then, I decided to go to Israel.

I boarded my first flight since arriving in New York to Tel Aviv in June 2022, marking a return to foreign travel after four months of being grounded. Zoe's summer school break had just begun so she was traveling with me.

For many people, a four-month pause in travel might seem perfectly normal, but for me, it felt unusual. I was used to jet-setting, often splitting my time between Moscow, New York, and many international cities. The only other time in recent years when I'd not traveled for a long time was during Covid-19. I flew to the Holy Land, thrilled to reunite with my team. We forged a collaboration with the Tel Aviv Dance Festival, supporting the program of young Israeli choreographers. I also co-produced several works by Israeli choreographers for European festivals. In addition, we created an audiowalk performance in Tel Aviv with the prestigious European company Rimini Protokoll.

Throughout that summer, my team and I were actively involved in pitching, workshops, and master classes in Israel. While these projects were exciting, they felt small compared to what we used to accomplish. Thankfully, though, they kept us afloat until the end of 2022.

My friend from Moscow also came to Tel Aviv. We talked — a lot. I told her everything about my new life. She listened and then said, "I know you're doing this for your kids, but you shouldn't be so hard on yourself. And you know you can still come back home right? You can stay at my place if you want." It might sound sentimental, but to me, that promise meant everything. Even when life pulled you apart through dramatic events, it was powerful to know that true friendship was everlasting — that someone was keeping you close in thought, feeling, and understanding.

Zoe stayed in Israel with her dad for the first time since the war began. My son was visiting his dad as well, so I was on my own.

I headed to the Stuttgart Festival with Lisa Rosov. Officially, she was the programming director of the MART Foundation, but to me, she was much more than that. Lisa has been by my side for over ten years, playing a crucial role in everything I've built. She's sharp, reliable, and deeply committed. With a mother who is one of the world's top ballet teachers, she grew up with dance — first as a ballet dancer herself, but like me, she eventually found her true passion in contemporary dance productions.

We were co-producers of Shahar Binyamini's work — a renowned Israeli choreographer — for the Stuttgart Dance Festival. It was fun, but my back was killing me, probably from all the stress I'd been feeling. I'd heard there was a masseuse in Baden-Baden, Germany, just about an hour away, so I rented a car and drove there. It seemed like a good idea to find a place to relax and take a bit of a breather. To return to the metaphor of the smart horse — it was time to get off the new track and rest.

After the doctor's visit my back pain and mood lifted, and I felt ready to explore. I googled "What is Baden-Baden famous for?" First, parks and gardens came up. It seemed to me that panoramic hiking trails and walks in the fresh air were just what I needed. Second, the town was renowned for its old casino. The world-famous Russian writer Fyodor Dostoevsky, who had always been my favorite novelist, spent some time in Baden-Baden and based the setting of his novel, *The Gambler*, on the town's casino. Last but not least, Baden-Baden was known for its thermal baths. I decided to give it a try. I was excited, but I didn't have a bathing suit. Inside the bathhouse, the receptionist told me not to worry, they would give me a sheet. I felt relieved, thinking I was off the hook. When I undressed and stepped into the first bathing room, a woman greeted me with a friendly Hallo! and promptly pulled the sheet away from me. I didn't see that coming. Therme Friedrichs bath had seventeen bathing stations, and you were supposed to spend about ten minutes in each before moving on to the next one. The entire experience was designed to take around three hours. Oh, and it was a mixed facility, where men and women used the space together at the same time, completely naked. I wasn't a puritan by any means, but I'd never been a nudist, so this was a surprise.

When I realized that I needed to spend a few hours naked with naked strangers, I wanted to run away, but the woman who took my sheet was staring at me, judging my decision, so I summoned my courage and stayed. Over the previous months, I'd heard many times how brave I was, so I thought I could probably handle it. But at first, that wasn't the case — I was sure I looked awful. When it comes to body-shaming, we are often our own worst enemy. I thought everyone was looking at me and judging my cellulite. I was too lazy to go to the gym, I didn't do Botox, and I had put on some extra weight since leaving Moscow.

Fifteen minutes later, though, I realized that people didn't care, because they were focused on enjoying themselves and the warm baths. Fifteen more minutes passed, and I began judging the women around me.

Now I was thinking, "I don't look terrible for my age; I'm actually quite okay." I was such an idiot. The last fifteen minutes of my visit were a blast. I finally managed to completely relax — it was just me enjoying the soothing thermal water.

Baden-Baden helped me learn a lesson surrounding how we tend to overcomplicate our lives. That healing spring water helped me regain a sense of myself. When I saw my reflection in a store window, I decided on the spur of the moment not to return the rental car and to continue my solo trip instead.

I found myself on the road driving to the Avignon Festival in France, one of the world's most important contemporary performing arts events. I loved this festival. A few years earlier, I was invited to be a co-producer of one of the plays that had the premier at Avignon. As soon as I made this plan, I felt a little closer to the old version of myself. Wow, think of that, I thought. I had a plan! Look at me — finally after months of worry and indecision wanting to do something and feeling excited about it.

To get to Avignon, I decided to drive through Germany, Switzerland, and Italy. Before going on the open road, I got a phone call from a friend in Washington, D.C. He told me I was totally insane to just go off like that, but then added, "Okay, but can you at least promise to keep me posted and let me know where you're going to spend the night?" I assured him I'd planned that too. "Am I a producer or what?" I joked. I wanted to visit some friends who were relocating to Europe from Moscow.

So my road trip began. First stop: Zurich, the city perched on a beautiful lake and ringed by valleys and hills. I parked the car and spent a few hours by the water near St. Peter's Church, watching swans drift across the lake as the sun began to set, my favorite time of day. This calm stirred up unexpected thoughts about the war, humanity, and how, as a society, we were failing our kids. Why were we so cruel? What would happen to my homeland, Russia, after this war? And what would come of those who were against it or supported it, or of places like Switzerland that seemede to avoid taking a side?

I decided to leave as I'd planned to spend the night with my friends, the Rodnyanskys. Alexander — a renowned Ukrainian film producer — and his wife Valeria had been my close friends for years.

I first learned about Alexander Rodnyansky through his documentaries while working on my diploma at the university. I was nineteen, and he was already a successful filmmaker and producer who had launched a TV channel in Ukraine. I met him in person in Moscow while working on the concept for my Documentary Film Center, and he was eager to support me. We became friends, and now our children are good friends too. The last time I'd seen Rodnyansky was before the war in Moscow, where we had lunch near my house and discussed potential collaboration. Somehow we touched upon citizenship — despite having lived in Russia for many years and launching several successful projects, he didn't have a Russian passport. He actually said he never wanted one. This stuck in my mind, and I recalled it a month later when the war broke out.

I drove to their house in Italy, where they had settled at the time. The drive took nearly three hours, so I downloaded Erich Maria Remarque's *Arch of Triumph*. It turned out to be one of the best decisions I'd made in months. If you asked me to name my top three writers, I'd say Remarque would be number two. His anti-war novels led Nazi propaganda minister Joseph Goebbels to label him as "unpatriotic." Remarque managed to escape to Switzerland and later to the United States, but his fame came at a heavy price — his sister, who remained in Germany, was executed by the Nazis.

Driving through Switzerland, I kept thinking about how people can feel like outsiders in their own country, just as they do in a foreign one. That was exactly how I felt — lost and like nobody really understood me. I got it — people were mad and traumatized and took it out on those who left. But at the same time, those who left didn't really have each other's backs. Only when someone passed away did people realize how great they were. I guess I wasn't exactly easy to like either. People saw me as privileged, so there wasn't much empathy for me. When I started over in a new country, I still tried to help others whenever I could, but I felt limited in what I could do. I was careful with my words about people who stayed, not wanting to hurt anyone. And yet, so many Russians seemed to turn against me.

When I shared this feeling with Rodnyansky, he said something that comforted me: "People will become aggressive toward you because they can't forgive your bravery in being vulnerable. It truly takes guts to leave a good life behind and start from scratch," he told me. "They maybe wanted to do it themselves, but they were too afraid to take that step."

That may be so, I said, but maybe that bravery wasn't what it seemed. I told Rodnyansky that I had no idea what to do with my life. I needed a stable job, I needed money — I was practically raising two kids on my own, alone in a new country. What should I do? Should I start a ballet school or maybe open a manicure salon? Cosmetic services weren't great in New York. Or perhaps I should return to the touring business or get involved in theater? Maybe I should write a book — or something else entirely?

He encouraged me to try everything — whatever came to mind — and to keep pushing forward until something finally clicked.

Two days later, I continued my road trip and drove to the Avignon Festival, where my friend Kirill Serebrennikov was presenting his play *The Black Monk*. Serebrennikov was a Russian theater and film director known for his bold, often controversial works. He built one of the best modern theater companies in Russia, Gogol Center, which was famous for tackling both political and social issues in its stage productions. Serebrennikov faced legal challenges in Russia, drawing attention to the struggles of artists under government pressure. He was under house arrest for more than a year and left Russia as soon as he got his passport back, just a few months before the war. I loved his theater works. In July 2019, I co-produced his first play for the Avignon Festival, *Outside,* which explored censorship and friendship. It was very well received. So I knew his team, his actors. I hadn't seen them in a while, but I wasn't in the mood for celebrations and only briefly congratulated everyone on their success.

Visiting the festival and watching those plays planted a thought in me: If I want to do something, first, I should produce a play. It shouldn't be something light and festive, but something born out of what hurts me, what eats me alive from the inside.

As I continued my journey, I kept thinking about something John Steinbeck wrote in *Travels With Charley* — "People don't take trips, trips take people." That's exactly how I felt. This wasn't just travel; it was something bigger, with a shift brewing inside me.

While I was on that trip, I got a call from a friend back in Moscow. She told me to keep quiet — don't talk publicly about the war, don't donate to Ukraine's defense, don't post about it for god's sake. Honestly, it wasn't even the first time someone had warned me. Friends, colleagues… people would drop subtle hints, basically telling me to shut up. But I couldn't. I kept speaking out anyway, posting some information on my Instagram page even after it was banned in Russia not long after the war started. Why? I don't know, I wasn't that famous and I didn't expect that my words could change anything. Maybe I simply didn't want to be silent, I just could not be seen as a Switzerland. Maybe I was simply afraid that, years from now, when my children asked me what I did when the war began, my only answer would be that I did nothing — that I stayed silent out of fear.

At some point, I found out the authorities had opened a temporary military draft office right next door to my Documentary Film Center. I mean, come on! The DFC had always been about independent films and free thinking. One of the last major festivals

I organized at DFC before the war was *American Fall*, showcasing a collection of 1970s American films. That era, marked by relaxed censorship, allowed filmmakers like Scorsese, Altman, and Coppola to push boundaries and tackle bold, unfiltered themes. The festival was a powerful showcase of creative freedom, and the audience's reaction was electrifying! It was all possible just a few months earlier ... and now there's a place sending kids to war right beside it?

It felt like our doors were closing, and theirs — the ones pushing propaganda, justifying lies — opening wide. It was hard to take. Since I wasn't cooperative, the authorities soon came up with a fabricated excuse about the building's fire safety operations and shut us down completely. A few months later, a few people from the movie industry took over my DFC. They moved into the space I had created and built from scratch without any doubts or issues. They supported the government and the war, and problems with the fire safety department disappeared.

Little by little, all my ties to Russia started breaking. My mom and some friends were still in Moscow, but beyond that I was done with my homeland. The good thing? When all this was going down, I wasn't holed up alone in some sad rental. I was on the road, with Remarque as my companion, glancing at the Mediterranean Sea in the side mirror and already dreaming of what I'd do once I got back to New York. On my way from Avignon to the airport, I'd formulated a plan: I would produce a play — something about hate, war, love, and life with all our complexities and weaknesses. That first trip abroad was the start of my spiritual rebirth as I embarked on this journey in my new home and country.

Sofia Kapkov with her kids — Anastasia, Ivan,
and Zoe. Moscow, November 2020

Sofia Kapkov at the Documentary Film
Center (DFC). Moscow, 2020

Sofia Kapkov and Alexander Rodnyansky at the DFC at the opening of the American Autumn Film Festival. November 2021

Gala during dance festival "Diana Vishneva."
St. Petersburg, November 2017

Opening night for "Autodance" by Sharon Eyal,
produced by MART. Moscow, April 2021

MART Festival in Tel Aviv, produced by
Sofia Kapkov. February 2020

Gala by Gogol Center, co-produced by
MART. Tel Aviv, March 2020

Young artists opera programme by Bolshoy Theater. Tour
to Tel Aviv, produced by Sofia Kapkov. March 2020

Premiere of the play *The Black Monk* by Kirill
Serebrennikov. Avignon Festival, July 2022

After the premiere of the play *Outside* by Kirill Serebrennikov
at Avignon festival, co-produced by MART.

Kirill Serebryannikov, Sofia Kapkov, and
Akram Khan. Moscow, 2019

Chapter 6

In September 2022, Zoe and Ivan started the new school year. Ivan just turned sixteen, and this was his final school year. He was incredibly smart, and due to the change in school systems, he skipped a grade, making this year his last. In just two months, we were planning to start the university application process. As you can imagine, even in a typical situation, this can be a nerve-wracking time for both students and parents. Given everything we'd been through, it was an especially anxious period.

When it came to Zoe, I didn't anticipate many issues, but I was caught off guard when I received an email informing me that she would have a new teacher and be placed in a different class. This was another of the many differences that arose when you moved to a new country. In Russia, when a child starts elementary school, they have the same teacher for at least four years, meaning the same teacher, the same classmates, and the same class. In contrast, in the U.S., kids switch teachers and classmates every year.

Honestly, I've come to prefer the American system. I believe it offers more opportunities for kids to adapt, meet new people, and develop important social skills while they're young. In the Russian system, however, kids stay with the same group, and as they get older, they don't always have the social skills needed to easily meet new people or make friends.

So when I received that email about Zoe's new teacher and class, I was initially concerned. But I was relieved to learn that she liked her new teacher and, as always, made new friends without any trouble.

I wasn't asking much from life at that point. Months passed fast without any significant break-throughs. I struggled to adjust to time not moving as quickly as I was used to. I knew I wanted to produce a play, but everything I came across felt too obvious or too simple. Nothing sparked that sense of purpose I was craving and that came to me with such power on my road trip in Europe.

My mantra at that time was to fake it until you make it, so I pretended everything was okay. When my mom called, I told her we were good; when friends asked how I was doing, I learned to respond without saying anything. I met new people, but small talk in New York still felt unnatural. In Moscow, people thought I was antisocial, that I was a snob looking down on everyone. Here, I wasn't even interested in myself. I didn't want anyone to know I was from Moscow. When someone asked where I was from, I simply said I lived in New York. Guilt and anger churned within me, and although I thought that I'd had a breakthrough during that trip to Europe, I hadn't yet figured out how to calm those feelings when they welled up in me.

I started getting offers to work with Russians again. I turned them down not only because of the political turmoil of the war but also because I didn't believe in any of these ideas. Although I needed money, I still received alimony from Zoe's father, but it barely covered my daughter's expenses in one of the most expensive cities in the world. I updated my CV, which I hadn't touched since my twenties, and created a LinkedIn account but ended up only having a few unsuccessful job interviews. Yet my dark moods had more to do with creative stagnation than money worries. Sofia, the creator of projects I used to call "my babies," was gone. What once made me proud and triumphant felt degrading now, as if it reduced my entire identity to something small and unimportant.

Depression set in that fall as I felt utterly lonely and stuck. My son still struggled to cope with the move, and on top of that, I lost close friends. We simply stopped talking to each other. I didn't know friendship could be so elusive. There was one person I considered a close friend for many years, and I genuinely believed that we saw the world through a similar lens. With another person, our bond was more about spending social time and having fun together. It turned out that immigration reshaped many things, including friendships. When you're caught up in the daily struggles of life, you often don't have the time or emotional energy to deal with unnecessary personal drama.

Looking back, I wonder if we were ever truly friends or if it was simply a matter of convenience for both of us. When that convenience faded, so did the connection. I was heartbroken when the fallout happened. I still blame myself for it and regret that we couldn't hold on to the intimacy and trust we once had.

Eventually it got to the point that I lost almost all contacts with my previous social network. Some people were offended by my social media activities; others thought I was judging them for not leaving Russia the way I had. A few simply gave up on me, being too caught up in their new lives, which seemed far more fun and exciting than whatever I had going on. One person told me I was tone-deaf, another that I had betrayed all my friends. When I tried to explain myself, it only made them angrier. It was hard to take. So my life got narrower and narrower, until I felt myself closing off.

At that time, my routine looked like this: I woke up at 6:00 a.m., made porridge for my daughter's breakfast, and packed her lunchbox for school. After dropping her off, I returned home to wake up my son — a daily struggle, as he never wanted to go to school. It was tough. I had to push him out the door and make sure he actually got on the school bus.

One day, I was so doubtful that he'd go that I jumped on the same bus just to be sure. His school was only three stops away. At some point, he decided to change his seat and ended up sitting near me — almost directly across from where I was. But he didn't notice me. I was right there, and yet somehow I was invisible. At that moment, I thought, "This is who I am now — nobody. Invisible. Unremarkable. Unnoticed."

Later, if I had the energy, I'd take a walk in Central Park. After that, I'd meditate, as it was the only thing keeping me somewhat sane. I took a transcendental meditation course eight years ago. Like many people, I was a fan of David Lynch, and since he was such a strong advocate for this form of mediation, I decided to give it a try. It turned out to be one of the best investments I'd ever made in myself.

I might have a few Zoom calls after that, do some vacuuming, and then make lunch. After picking up my daughter in the early afternoon, I'd take her to ballet or gymnastics. I felt thoroughly lost. For many years, one of my favorite colors was gray: a reflection of the uncertain. Now all my life slowly turned into a gray area itself. This was so unlike the old me who was typically blooming, brimming with projects, and energizing others.

Nine months in New York felt like an eternity. Besides, the older you get, the more you appreciate time. I was feeling a waste of my days without a clear plan to move forward.

All my life, I battled migraines. I tried everything — Western medicine, Chinese herbs, ancient remedies. Nothing helped. When I moved to New York, the stress made everything worse. I took whatever pills I could find, but nothing really worked.

One day, something happened that I'll never forget. It was a gray, rainy November day. I had a migraine so bad I could barely stand. Zoe had Covid and a high fever. Ivan was sick too. I was alone, in terrible pain, and too weak to call for help. And honestly, who would I call? My oldest daughter? I didn't want to drag her into this. I gave the kids Tylenol — at least, I think I did — and eventually, they fell asleep. I collapsed on the bathroom floor, next to the toilet, vomiting and shaking. Around 4:00 a.m., I remember crying and saying to myself, *I can't take this anymore. I can't live like this.* After that, I must have passed out or fallen asleep. When I woke up a few hours later, the migraine was gone. I checked Zoe — her fever was gone too. Morning light was coming through the window. I thought, "I survived. I made it. I can do this." But I also knew I needed help. I called my daughter and told her, "I think I have depression. I need to see a doctor. I need to start taking antidepressants."

I want to say something here: Depression is a very serious disease. If you feel it or notice that someone you love shows signs of it, you need to seek help immediately. There is no shame in asking for help. I was born and raised in a society where phrases like "oh, you don't look depressed" or "don't be depressed" were thrown around like jokes or seen as signs of weakness. I think it's extremely dangerous that some people still view it that way.

My personal experience with antidepressants wasn't great, so I'm choosing not to share the details in this book. I want to keep that part private. I also don't want anyone to feel influenced to copy my journey, because every person's experience is different.

However, there is one thing I do recommend without hesitation: Please, see a doctor. Professional help can make all the difference.

The doctor's appointments were helpful for me. As well as the meetings with the same friend from D.C. who suggested I visit my daughter at the beginning of the war. He went from being just an acquaintance to a very close friend. He checked on me twice a day, every day. He came back to New York after two weeks since that terrible migraine episode. He found me very upset, sat me down, and we talked for a few hours. In that talk, something he said stuck with me.

He said, "I remember you from our first lunch in London. You were such a cold, arrogant Siberian bitch, but I sat there looking at you with admiration and desire. You gave me the impression that you could run the world. You were smart, beautiful, independent, creative, and full of life and energy. I am a hustler so I can recognize another when I see it. It's still inside you. Imagine living in a vast ocean, like a fish swimming through the water. You knew everything in that ocean, you knew everyone, and you swam everywhere. Everything was amazing, and you were successful. Then, for some reason, you were thrown onto dry land. All those qualities — your speed, your talent — are still inside you. You just happened to end up on land. It's really hard and challenging, but I'm sure you'll succeed here too. You just need to learn to move on land. Instead of moving, you're standing at the water's edge, checking the temperature of the ocean. Because of that, you're not making any progress. As you are not making any progress, you feel so bad about yourself. As soon as you start making progress on land, you will feel better, and, more importantly, you might be able to come back anytime and help more people. But you have to stop checking the temperature and start moving."

For me, that was a huge WOW! I suddenly felt the way I did at the psychology session, like my friend had unlocked me from this brand-new prison that circumstances had conspired to throw me into.

That talk with my friend at the end of November 2022 was just what I needed to shake me from my obsession of starting each day reading about war and Russia. Every morning, like many other people, while my kids were still sleeping, I spent hours diving straight into that news, starting with updates from Russia before flipping through *The New York Times* from cover to cover. Later during the day, I got back to all depressing and upsetting news and Telegram Channels. I decided I had to change that routine, that I must stop living in the past and instead focus on my future. It took a lot of discipline, but here's what I did: I deleted Facebook completely from all devices and took a break from reading the news feeds from my Russian friends. I cleaned up my Instagram, removed a lot of people who had stayed in Moscow and were posting every day about their peaceful and successful lives in Moscow, sharing about parties, new restaurants, and movie premieres. On top of that, I unsubscribed from all my Telegram Channels. Not because the world out there was evil, not because their happiness was a lie, but because my space needed to be cleaned and cleared. Little by little, day by day, my mood and my life in New York started to change.

It had taken ten months since I arrived in New York that fateful day in February 2022, but finally I found my old self reviving. I pulled myself out of that mental fog, and took action, signing up for one of the most popular classes at Yale University, The Science of Well-Being, in a bid to keep my dark moods at bay and incorporated some of that practice into my routine. I began practicing transcendental meditation twice a day for twenty minutes, waking every morning, and keeping a diary. I used to write in a diary before the war as well, occasionally writing down my thoughts or important events in my life. I decided to be disciplined about it, and I put everything that happened to me into my journal. If walking helped me calm down, writing helped me think clearly. I also thought it might be useful for my children — or maybe even my grandchildren — to read about how their mother once lived.

I was determined to follow that path I'd thought about back in those Baden-Baden days, and finally was making room in my mind for new dreams that would lead to opportunities. Though as a person who believed in the promise of failing better, I knew they didn't just fall from the sky.

Chapter 7

Once I began feeling better, I started talking to people and browsing for the kind of material I wanted to devote my energies to. I didn't have a clear vision of what I was going to do, but I wanted to produce a play that reflected all my feelings and thoughts about what was going on in the world. I'd never done anything like that before. First of all, I wasn't familiar with the American theater — the rules, policies, and overall way of doing things were completely new to me. Second, I'd never produced a play from scratch on my own, even in Russia. Of course, I had some general idea of how theater worked there, but that was it. For some reason, I just believed I was capable of doing it.

I read a lot of plays and scripts, but nothing felt like the right fit. I found myself constantly reflecting on how people who were so similar and lived nearby could possibly pick up guns and kill each other without even asking themselves, "Why am I doing this?"

Then, one night, I had a dream. I dreamed of a school on the border between Ukrainian Kharkiv and Russian Belgorod, where all classmates were speaking Russian, reading Pushkin, and sharing all holidays together. Suddenly these two neighboring cities were caught in the war, and its citizens, infected with hate, began killing each other. When I woke up I almost screamed. *Oh, my God!* I thought. After spending so much time searching and looking into everything, here it was. I had to produce *Our Class* in New York, a place where I knew it had never been staged before.

Our Class was a play written by renowned Polish playwright Tadeusz Slobodzianek about ten Polish classmates — five Jewish and five Catholic — who grew up as friends and neighbors and then turned on one another with life-or-death consequences. The play was inspired by real-life events surrounding a horrific 1941 pogrom in a small Polish village, Jedwabne, and based on the book *Neighbors* by Princeton professor Jan Gross. I knew about this play. *Our Class* had been staged in fifteen different versions worldwide, including one that was running at the Moscow Vakhtangov Theater. In 2020, I took this show on tour to Israel as a producer, and I was even discussing bringing the play to America.

When the war began, the theater's director called me and mentioned they were open to coming to the U.S., but first I had to confirm that we would send a donation for a "special operation" (what the war was called in Russia). I, of course, refused, telling him it was impossible, and added that I had emigrated to America. I had completely forgotten about the play until I had the fateful dream about the school on the border between Kharkiv and Belgorod.

The next morning, I called my friend, the playwright and director in Poland, Ivan Vyrypaev. I asked if he could help me get in touch with Tadeusz Slobodzianek. He gave me his email address, and I reached out to Tadeusz right away. I introduced myself: "My name is Sofia Kapkov, I'm a producer living in New York, and I left Russia after the war erupted. I know your play very well and want to produce it, as it has never been staged in New York." I wrote the email in Russian as I knew he could read it in Russian. Tadeusz responded in Polish the next day, and I managed to read it with the help of Google Translate. He said it was his dream to have a show in New York.

I didn't have any money to produce the play, but I explained that I would fundraise and was sure I would find the way to stage it. I told Tadeusz this play had a personal itch for me — the need to express my own pain and grapple with my questions about the war and the hatred among people. I wanted to release everything that was bubbling and hissing inside me like a volcano. In that sense, I saw myself as a creative producer who must feel that intensity and pain — didn't matter what it is — to take on something remarkable like *Our Class*.

I also didn't have a director, actors, or a potential venue. The most important step was finding a director.

I had one candidate in mind, so I called him right away, but he said he wasn't interested. Given what happened next, I suppose you could say that everything happens for a reason.

On December 6, I had a scheduled meeting with Sara Stackhouse, a theater producer from Boston. We had only met once before on Zoom. She wanted to meet me in person since she was in New York. She had heard a lot about my activities in Israel and wanted to know my opinion about a play that her partner, Igor Golyak, had done with Mikhail Baryshnikov. They were considering taking it on tour to Israel. I mentioned I wasn't sure I could help because of budget considerations, but I said I would be happy to meet. Honestly, though, I wasn't. I still didn't feel comfortable meeting in person with a successful American producer. I was very unhappy with the weakness of my English, which made every meeting feel like a struggle.

We met in a French brasserie on the Upper East Side, and instead of the planned forty-five minutes, we ended up talking for about two hours. Fun fact: I now live near that restaurant and every time I walk past it I remember our first conversation.

Sara was a bit late, and I'm always on time. When she arrived, she had a big purse overflowing with a computer, shoes, and other items, along with a suitcase. I was surprised because she wasn't what I had expected.

Now that I know her well, I realize she doesn't care much about first impressions. I, on the other hand, still worry about how people perceive my appearance, but I'm afraid that doesn't help, as more people seem to like her more than me when they first meet us. Sara was incredibly nice and sweet, paying no attention to my English, accent, or any language mistakes that I made. We discussed the play with Baryshnikov, and then she asked me about my move to New York.

I shared my story, and she looked very impressed. She said I should write a book about it one day. She also told me that I was brave and strong. I said that I didn't see myself as strong. Resilient, yes, but not necessarily strong. She then shared her story. Born and raised in Massachusetts, her first summer job was babysitting for the child of a famous musician, who liked her so much that he offered her a full-time position as his assistant and producer after she graduated from college.

Sara produced numerous tours, working at a Shakespeare company for years. In the previous five years, she dedicated her life to the Arlekin Players Theater and her partner, director Igor Golyak, focusing primarily on doing projects in the Boston area. She mentioned that she met Igor while managing a department at the Boston Conservatory, where she had planned to hire him to teach the art of theater. She was surprised that she had never heard of the theater he was directing, especially since she had lived in Boston her whole life. After attending his performance in a tiny, sold-out house — which, by the way, was in Russian, a language she couldn't understand — she was left stunned by the show. She immediately recognized that his talent deserved more recognition and needed to be seen. So she invited him to collaborate, and together they formed a partnership, with Sara leaving her job to become his managing producer.

When Covid-19 hit, Igor found himself stuck at home. Creative people were going stir-crazy with theaters shut down and with no way to perform. Driven by the urge to make art, he decided to create a live performance. People began sharing links with one another, and *The New York Times* featured it as a "groundbreaking development in theater," recognizing Igor as a "leading innovator of virtual theater." The legend Mikhail Baryshnikov also received the link and was so impressed that he offered to collaborate with him. That's how the Orchard Project was born, featuring a futuristic robot on stage with Baryshnikov performing as Firs and Anton Chekhov.

I thought her story was no less impressive than mine. She wanted me to meet Igor but said he was busy and wasn't able to join us. Many months later, when Igor and I had built a strong relationship, we had a talk after one of our shows. Someone asked him about the war. Igor replied, "I was born in Kyiv, Ukraine, and moved to America at the age of eleven. It's very difficult for me, Russian culture is a part of my identity. I speak Russian, I studied at Moscow theater school, but I hate Russia so much right now." With me being a producer from Russia, I guess it wasn't just a busy schedule that kept him from meeting with me and Sara on that day.

When we asked for the check, Sara wanted to know my secret. I replied that I didn't have any, besides the fact that I truly believed everything will be okay in the end; if it's not okay, it's not the end. I also said I'm always holding on to a dream that keeps me alive.

"What's your new dream?" she asked.

I said I wanted to produce a play in New York.

"What play?"

Channeling my inner snobby Russian, I replied, "Oh, you know, I don't think you're familiar with it. It's never been produced on Broadway; it has more of a European theater vibe." In retrospect, it was such a stupid response! I still blush when I remember that moment. Sara didn't even blink; she simply said, "Try me." I said, "*Our Class*."

"Oh my God!" Sara exclaimed. "Unbelievable! Igor has told me so many times about this play; he wanted to direct it. You need to meet him." She texted him right away. I don't know what she said to him exactly, but the next day, the three of us met. As I was already looking for the play's director and Igor not only knew about *Our Class* but wanted to direct it, I thought it was not just a coincidence but quite a positive sign from the universe!

I started sharing my ideas for *Our Class*. I said how relevant it felt, explained why it was important for me, and added I was ready to invest myself in it. I said I wanted to make the play not about something terrible that happened to Jews in the past, but something contemporary — about what my country is doing right now: neighbors killing neighbors. What haunted me most was how we would live with it afterward. In *Our Class*, that was exactly what happened: Those who raped and killed kept living, carrying those memories quietly through the years, until they died. This play wasn't just about a tragedy — it was about how life goes on after, and how the past never really leaves.

Igor agreed with my ideas and shared what he had in mind. He was Jewish, so that also ticked a box for the play. He was also seeing how it was relevant in the United States, which was becoming increasingly divided day by day. He said, "I want to make a play about something that is about to happen." Little did we know how even more relevant it would become after the Hamas attack on Israel on October 7, 2023, which brought a whole new level of meaning and global significance to our play.

The next day, I wrote to Tadeusz that I had found an incredibly talented director, and we arranged a Zoom call. Tadeusz could understand Russian as Poles of his age had learned the language during the days of Soviet control. He asked us which of the many English translations of *Our Class* we liked the most. We had read all five and had settled on Norman Allen's version, which turned out to be his favorite too.

In two weeks, I bought the rights to stage the play in New York. Tadeusz's agent was tough and wanted more money, but I couldn't accept that offer. Finally, he agreed to our unusual proposal to give me the rights not for the whole country, but for a few cities, including New York. Now that I had the rights and the director, it was time to start fundraising.

This was the kind of work that had always made me feel like I was doing something that actually mattered. It wasn't just about the task itself; it was about seeing my own power in it, knowing that I was creating something real and important for myself and others. It is that feeling of accomplishment that sets me free.

Chapter 8

American culture cultivates a strong principle of giving, with most wealthy people dedicating a portion of their wealth to charities. This donation is also tax deductible, meaning that charitable giving can lower the income tax expense. What's more, New York has more millionaires than any other city in the world, with one in every twenty-four residents, based on a Bloomberg report in 2024.

In addition, New York has the biggest population of Jewish people in the U.S. and a large number of Russian-speaking communities. So I was certain that I was in the right city to raise money for *Our Class*.

My U.S.-based nonprofit, MART Foundation, is the organization I lead to support contemporary performing arts programs globally. Before *Our Class*, we premiered shows in France; presented projects at Carnegie Hall in New York, Sadler's Wells, and the Barbican Centre in London; and backed dance festivals including those in Tel Aviv, Stuttgart, and the Netherlands.

Our mission has always been to bring forth projects of cultural significance and to showcase artists I was proud of. For instance, we were the first to organize a tour for Leonid Desyatnikov, one of the last great composers from Russia alive today. Despite his stature, at nearly seventy years old, he had never received state support for an international tour. So we took him to London, Israel, and even the world-renowned Carnegie Hall, creating a memorable tour. It was truly stunning. We've also co-produced with American companies; when interests aligned, we'd step in and offer support. This has allowed us to build bridges and foster cross-border collaborations.

Even though I was new to New York, I'd built a reputation as a reliable producer among some people in the industry. Yet starting fundraising for a new project was always a fresh challenge. I'd met incredible philanthropists at evening galas, gallery openings, random gatherings, Shabbat dinners, and Sunday brunches and even once met a perfect person on a dating app, for goodness sake, but I needed much more than just to meet the person. I had to find the right one for my project — a sponsor specifically interested in my show.

I felt blessed to be back to being the person known as having the kind of infectious energy that inspired others. I loved being able to work with people and help them achieve their goals. That energy attracted donations from supporters and led to introductions to others who might also offer their support. In the end, though, it was a numbers game of knocking on doors. I just lived with an attitude that failure was not an option. Most potential donors would stay on the sidelines, but a few would inevitably say yes.

The first step we took for *Our Class* was to sit down with Sara and estimate the budget. Sara explained to me the difference between Broadway and off-Broadway productions, which differ in budget, scale of production, and the size of the theater. Budgeting was going to be a tricky task: To start with, we knew the show was going to have ten actors plus three understudies. Also, we needed a venue for rehearsal and the venues for a run, a costume designer, a composer, and a set designer. In addition, Igor's artistic approach was quite innovative, and all his shows included video and projections, so even if we didn't begin discussing the concept, we'd have to be ready to budget it just in case. What's more, there were royalties and technical crew, marketing expenses, including website and all promo materials and, in our case, travel expenses. From the beginning, we decided that Igor and a few members from the creative team had to go to Poland, to Auschwitz and Jedwabne, to meet people who still lived there and to see the place where people one day long ago burned their neighbors in the barn.

We were going to make it our own way without sacrificing the quality and the effect of the production for a lower budget. Experienced producers warned us that we were aiming to produce an off-Broadway play, applying Broadway standards to it, all while underestimating the budget. Our decision to use so many elaborate elements in an off-Broadway drama didn't align with what was typically done in New York theater, where it was believed you didn't need special effects or a large cast like you would for a big Broadway show. Quite often when you came to see an off-Broadway show, it was just two people on stage or two chairs.

Now I understand why that's the case. It's almost impossible to recoup the money when putting on a large-scale show on the smaller off-Broadway venue. You have to be innovative and creative to find new schemes and solutions. Every day, we faced issues that, if you treated this project just as work, you'd probably say, "Okay, I'm done. It's impossible."

But for Sara and me, it wasn't just a work project — it was our lives that we were putting on the line. For me, because I needed to start over with this chosen project, I felt that I couldn't afford to fail. Meanwhile, Sara felt that she had risked everything for Igor. So we relied on all our survival skills to get through each day, just to make it to the next. While we weren't aiming for Broadway, we wanted to prove that even with a limited audience, we could create a mesmerizing experience.

This approach was, in some way, counter-American. My initial contact with the Western way of doing things wasn't through theater, but rather through dance festivals and movie production. I recall one episode in 2011 when we were shooting a documentary about cancer in Los Angeles. We arrived at a major movie studio in Hollywood to conduct an interview. When we finished, our cameraman started coiling wires, which caused a stage manager assistant to rush over and say, "What are you doing? This isn't your job, we have an assistant here for this." Our guy said something like, "Oh, don't worry, it's okay, I can do many things," and received an unfriendly look.

Now, as a U.S.-based producer, I understand that many things are strictly regulated. This can be beneficial in a factory situation, but theater work is more complicated. In Russia and Europe, at least where I had worked, the director was the key figure, someone akin to God. The whole theater worked around him, and their job was to create, hopefully, a spectacular production. The entire theater relied on the director, as a successful show sometimes ran for years.

But in the States, it's different. The director's role doesn't rise above that of the actor, producer, or stage manager. Everyone is treated equally. The director does their work, and so do the others. I think, within certain boundaries, the director should be treated like God, because that's how the best creative work is made. However, directors in the U.S. must abide by many rules, some of which — like the one that prohibits a director to give notes after the premiere to the cast — seem ridiculous to me. Instead, any notes must go through the stage manager, who continues working with the cast. Back in Russia, I preferred seeing performances about a week after the premiere; by then, the actors had usually warmed up and settled into their roles. But here I started attending shows early in the run, while the director was still around to adjust and guide the actors. Or another example: How could you navigate the process of creating movements if you were not allowed to touch dancers? Words alone can't capture the essence of what you're trying to achieve. It's not as simple as it seems.

Protocols surrounding unions and actors also can pose hurdles. On one hand, unions enforced a level playing field for actors. But that can seem unfair for talented and ambitious actors who can't earn more even when they work harder than the rest of the cast. In reality, it brings more restrictions and makes the work harder, and often the result of this work is very sad. Just recently, here on set, we needed something printed, but the printer wasn't working for some reason — whoever was supposed to maintain it hadn't done their job. The director said, "I need the script for rehearsal," but the staff member simply responded that it wasn't their job: "Someone else will come tomorrow and fix it."

That's the kind of attitude I have a hard time tolerating here in New York. It is not my intention to pass judgment; rather, I offer an observation drawn from experience. One of the most striking differences between American theater and what we call Russian theater lies in the attitude toward the profession itself. In the Russian tradition — especially after the Revolution and throughout the Soviet era — theater was regarded as sacred, almost like a secular church. To work in the theater was to be part of a mission: to elevate, to educate, to awaken the soul of the people. It was not simply a career — it was destiny. Directors such as Stanislavsky, Meyerhold, and later even figures like Efros or Dodin, were seen as priestly. Actors were expected to sacrifice for the sake of art; personal comfort was a distant second. In America, theater often operates within a capitalist framework. It remains an art, but it is inextricably entangled with business — shows have budgets, schedules, unions, rights, regulated hours. There is a sharper division between "work" and "life." Many young Americans today have grown up without the same sense of existential urgency. The prevailing attitude is more often: "This is my job, not my entire life." It is not that Americans lack passion for art — far from it — but the culture does not demand the same kind of total devotion. For many in America, theater is an industry: a form of employment not unlike working at a hospital, an office, a grocery store, or a factory. It is approached with the same professional expectations: Work begins at a set hour, ends at a set hour, and remains carefully cordoned off from private life. In this context, theater is a job. But for us — for many Russians — theater was never merely a profession; it was a calling. Directors were revered, often treated as gods. Actors surrendered themselves wholly to their craft, sometimes to the point of self-sacrifice. This devotion forged a culture where theater was not just entertainment or business, but a way of living and thinking — an essential part of a higher human purpose.

This is not to suggest that such a system was without its flaws; no environment built on such intensity can be free of problems. Yet the commitment it inspired was undeniable, creating an artistic atmosphere charged with seriousness and passion. This cultural gap sometimes gave rise to misunderstandings. When you come from a tradition where theater demands total dedication, it can be difficult to explain to someone raised in another system why you expect more than mere professional participation — why you seek passion, sacrifice, and a sense of belonging to something greater than oneself.

I'm still more inclined to work with people who come from a different school of thought, like that in Russia where I know that theater is something sacred, not just a job. In that environment, costume designers wouldn't say they couldn't finish a costume because their shift was over. They would keep working until the job was done because it was essential to the overall production.

When the White House in Moscow was stormed during the 1993 coup, the late famous director Pyotr Fomenko was holding a rehearsal at his theater right across from it. Tanks were everywhere. Someone ran into the theater to tell him what was happening, to which he quickly responded, "Please be quiet, we're rehearsing right now." Nothing could stop his rehearsals.

Chapter 9

Another big difference between Russian and American theater is funding. In Russia, most theaters are financially supported by the government. In the United States, theatrical companies have to hustle for every dollar. I never worked for an established theater in Russia, I was an independent producer, so I had to hustle and find my own funding. Funding comes in various, sometimes unexpected, forms. As a nonprofit, a straightforward route is to apply for grants. Attending charity events can spark someone's interest in your project. Once you secure a partnership with one foundation, it often becomes easier to engage others. Some will simply follow suit. For instance, when working on our Israeli dance project, we connected with choreographer Or Schraiber. I reached out to him and invited him to work on some movements for *Our Class*. Through him, we planned to find new supporters and donors who had previously backed his dance projects. Or did an outstanding job and was later nominated for Best Choreographer for his work for *Our Class*.

Our biggest challenge was timing. I was stressed, constantly wondering how quickly I could raise money.

While I knew who to approach for funding in Russia, I understood it would take more time and effort in the United States. Committing to a larger budget wasn't feasible, so we focused on the minimum we could realistically manage. According to a well-known theater producer, a budget for what we wanted would be around $2 million. Our first estimate was half a million, but we aimed to pull it off with just under $1 million. My responsibility was to to secure the first half during the next two months to kickstart the process.

Since the play primarily dealt with the mass murder of the Jewish community, I planned to approach our donors who support Israeli artists. By the end of January 2023, we had a beautifully crafted presentation deck. We outlined the venues we wanted, potential partnerships, ticket sales goals, our target audience, and media channels. It wasn't about having everything set but more about presenting our projections, our offer, and explaining our needs. I polished my pitch and started traveling with it.

While speaking to potential donors, I would mention that our director Igor was Jewish Ukrainian-American and that I had recently moved from Russia.

I had countless Zoom calls. Some were positive, many just a waste of time. I remember having a productive meeting with a foundation with Polish roots that supported Jewish inheritance. I was really looking forward to that partnership. At some point, Sara and I texted each other, feeling we'd hit the jackpot. "This is it! This is exactly what we need!" I said. But ultimately they turned us down, saying, "Unfortunately, we can't support you this time, as we believe the Poles will be represented in a way we don't want, and it will attract unnecessary attention."

I was upset and disappointed. I thought at least in America people were free to openly face controversial topics. I was hoping one day my motherland would be able to have such conversations about our terrible acts, not to cover up something that was done wrong or pretend that it never happened.

A few days later, we arranged a meeting in person with a Polish cultural institute in New York. I had another meeting at the same time and Sara could not be there on time. Honestly, we didn't expect much from the group, and so we sent my daughter, Anastasia, associate producer of *Our Class*, to the meeting. She was worried, but I said, "Listen, just be yourself, tell them everything about the project, you cannot fail us, we are one hundred percent sure they are not going to support us." In two hours she called us and declared: "The meeting went so well! The Polish institution is so excited and honored to be our partner, they promised to support us, promote the show, help with sales, and they can even give us a grant."

Sara and I were more than happy, and it was Anastasia's first solo victory. I was so proud of my girl and the young woman she had become. I had heard many great things about her work ethic, sense of responsibility, and dedication, but this was the first time I witnessed her professionalism firsthand. It made me dream that, perhaps one day, she might be interested in taking over my foundation.

When she was a child, I was going through divorce with her dad. I decided to consult a child therapist to be sure she was okay. The therapist spoke with both of us separately, and while Anastasia waited outside, he turned to me and said, "Sofia, you have great intuition. It's good that you came. Anastasia is fine. You two have the strong, loving bond a mother and daughter should have. The only thing is… in your relationship, the adult is Anastasia." She was only seven. I realized then I was the one who needed help.

I've been working on my own issues since then because, more than anything, I was afraid that I had failed as a mother and thus had made my children's lives miserable. I'm still a work in progress, trying to find the balance between being overprotective and giving them the freedom to live their own lives and learn from their mistakes. But when I see their victories, my heart fills with pride.

My first inclination after hearing the news was to call the donor who turned us down and say I'm glad not all Poles feel that what we were doing with *Our Class* would reflect badly on them, but I managed to keep that feeling to myself.

One never knows where you'll find good fortune. Years ago, while I was in Israel, I began learning Hebrew. I realized that if I wanted to truly connect with the country — especially to participate in festivals — I should at least try to learn the language. Plus, Hebrew was so beautiful. I took a hundred lessons, but didn't help, and I can still barely say a few sentences. Later in New York, I met a singer in a synagogue who agreed to become my language teacher. She connected me with her friends, and I was invited to beautiful Shabbat dinners. Everywhere I went, I was talking about this project. I simply couldn't talk about anything else, besides, you never know where you can meet potential sponsors.

We faced many rejections, mostly because the play wasn't seen as relevant enough. I explained that it was a contemporary piece about how neighbors — those sharing the same place, mindset, and culture — can end up killing each other. But at its core, it was still a Jewish play, set during the Holocaust in 1941. I'd heard so many times, "Sofia, it's such a terrible story and it's not relevant today."

When Hamas attacked Israel on October 7, 2023, we were still pulling the play together. People who had rejected us started calling me back, asking if I'd somehow anticipated this. Here we were, working on a play about Jewish people being murdered, about how we didn't want atrocities like this to happen to anyone. It was a surreal moment, and it hit home in a deeply personal way.

But that was then. Earlier that year, when we began applying for grants from foundations that might be interested, we approached about fifteen American funds that support theater, performing arts, or Jewish initiatives. Many of them turned us down before even meeting. It was a process: You send letters, presentations, hold Zoom calls, and then meet with your contacts. In those days when I was looking to raise half a million dollars, three foundations expressed interest right away and were ready to meet with me.

The first one was the Koum Family Foundation. This organization was established by my friend, Jan Koum, a brilliant and smart IT guy, who co-founded WhatsApp many years ago, a mobile messaging app that keeps so many people connected. The Koum Foundation supported a lot of social and cultural Jewish organizations. I sent the presentation and had a few conversations with Jan and his team. In the end, they agreed to support us if I managed to find other donors. Jan supported my projects through the years;

we established strong relations, but he could easily say no, and I am forever grateful that he said yes. He came to the premiere a year later and he looked happy and satisfied. I continue working with the Koum Foundation on other projects.

The Blavatnik Foundation was my second step. I flew to London to meet Len Blavatnik. His foundation was a well-known organization that, among other projects, supported arts initiatives with a Jewish focus. I hadn't worked with them before, but I knew Len socially. I sent an email, attached a presentation, and asked him to meet me. Blavatnik Foundation was renowned for backing some of the most prestigious nonprofits, including Lincoln Center and Carnegie Hall in New York. Len was known as a tough business-man who preferred to invest rather than donate. He asked me a lot of questions about the artistic approach, design, and potential future. After a while, he agreed to provide the initial funding. Unfortunately, he didn't come to the premiere and never saw the play but sent me a note with congratulations.

The last group was the Fooksman Family Foundation, which also supported many Jewish-related arts projects. I met Vita Anesh, the director of their fund, a few months after my arrival in New York, and she's one of my dear friends now. Vita was from Lviv and her husband was from Moscow, but they had lived in New York for many years. We shared a good friend in common who introduced us. Our kids went to the same school, and Vita immediately invited us to Shabbat. When I arrived, they welcomed me with an open heart. I felt like I was home again. We were neighbors, and the next morning she texted, "Please, open the door, we want to drop off a box with books in Russian for Zoe." Vita did so much for me: She introduced me to many people, Vita did so much for me. For one, she introduced me to her boss, Eugene Fooksman. When I was trying to find donors who could be interested in supporting *Our Class*. I sent her a deck, and she arranged the meeting in Manhattan. They brought three people from their office, and I came along. I talked about *Our Class*, hoping to impress them, especially since they had already seen the presentation.

By the end of the conversation, I was feeling enthusiastic — I had that gut feeling when you know the money is going to come through.

Then, for some reason, they asked me about my immigration. "What was the hardest part for you?" Eugene Fooksman asked, looking me in the eye.

I paused for a moment, then it hit me. "Imagine," I said, "you're married to someone, and over time, you experience all the ups and downs — the good and bad moments. Then, at some point, you realize your partner is not just a bad person, your partner is a pedophile. You ask yourself: 'How could I not have noticed this before? How could I have lived with someone like that?'" I thought it was the perfect way to metaphorically describe Vladimir Putin's Russia. I was devastated not just because of the country's leader, but the people who chose to trust him and his policies. That was exactly how I felt about Russians who supported the war. The support was indeed the hardest part for me, something that I just couldn't accept.

Later that same day, I received an email from Eugene — a positive response about how much he had enjoyed the meeting. It was official, yet emotional. The bottom line was that the foundation was happy to support the play and praised my bravery. I felt incredibly pleased and encouraged.

Two days later, I met with Vita. I mentioned how great I felt about the email I received from Eugene. She smiled and said, "You really left quite an impression." One woman who was at the meeting later shared her thoughts: "Sofia is so unique," she said. "Not only is she beautiful and young, but she's also accomplished so much, and left her country. On top of all that, her husband turned out to be a pedophile, and she was so honest about it."

Just for the record, I didn't have a pedophile husband! My English was just bad.

In any case, my speech worked. We had another supporter, and with that, the first half a million dollars was locked in. We opened a new bank account, hired the general manager, and the work began.

It wasn't all sunshine and rainbows along the way, of course. At later stages, we were close to landing a grant from another major philanthropic organization. Sara had applied through their Arlekin Players Theater. Everything seemed on track — they were enthusiastic and practically certain about awarding us the grant. But, as always, it came with endless paperwork, emails, and Zoom meetings. Then, right on the day of the premiere, they pulled out.

I've been told that the reason the deal fell through was that Arlekin Players is based in Boston, not in New York. We suggested receiving it through MART, but that meant they had to start the whole document process from scratch, which they were not willing to do. I was upset but didn't blame anyone for this at all because in this line of work, you're constantly sailing through stormy seas, battling one wave after another. If one door closes, don't stop — knock on another until it opens.

Chapter 10

In the winter of 2023, I was ready to put myself back out there and signed up for a dating app — something I'd never tried before. Back in Russia, there wasn't much need for it, but even if there was, I would never feel comfortable with using a dating app; the chances of running into someone I knew were way too high. In New York, after months of being single and feeling lonely, I felt it was the time; besides, I was an outsider. I was eager to dive into the uncharted world of dating, convincing myself it was also a chance to practice small talk and social skills while also getting to know Americans better.

There was another reason behind it: that valuable well-being course I took online at Yale. In addition to watching the lectures, the course required you to do the homework. Physical exercises and meditation had already become part of my daily routine, but participating in social life was much harder. For one week, one of the tasks was to engage in conversations with strangers. I decided that diving into the online dating world would help me achieve this goal. I couldn't fail, especially since earning my Well-being Certificate would confirm that I was officially on my way to becoming a happier person.

So I created my first dating app profile, and my new dating life began. On one date, I went out with a conductor from the Kennedy Center to watch *Tar*, a psychological drama with Cate Blanchett, and he introduced me to the world of conductors. Another date was less romantic, but the guy happened to be Jewish, and I spent the whole dinner pitching my project to him. He never asked for another date, but he donated a little bit and, in the end, probably blocked my number.

It was February 13, 2023, when a friend from D.C. came to visit me in New York. We went to lunch and he mentioned he would be back in the city in a couple of months. I filled him in on both my fundraising and what I considered my dating wins. He praised me for the fundraising, but for reasons that I didn't first understand, seemed skeptical about my dating hustle.

"Listen, I get it. But why are you going on all these ridiculous dates?" he asked.

"What's ridiculous about it? It's fun!" I said.

And then he bowled me over me with this — "Why don't you just go on a date with me?"

I blinked at him, completely thrown. "Why would we do that? We are friends," I said.

By then, we'd been tight-knit, confiding in each other like close friends do. I trusted him; I could tell him everything in my heart, and our conversations always calmed me down. After my response, he looked at me as if I'd said the dumbest thing imaginable and asked, "Are you blind, deaf, and clueless? Haven't you noticed anything? I have been patiently waiting for more than a year."

Stupid me, I hadn't noticed a thing — I guess I was too busy with all my problems and dreams. I said, "Okay, give me one good reason why I should go on a date with you." He looked me in the eyes and said, "If you go on a date with me, you're never going to leave me."

Wow, that was such an arrogant response. I laughed so hard, I almost choked. I said, "Okay, I'll be kind," and agreed to go on a date with him the next time he came to the city.

The next morning after I took Zoe to school, he texted me as usual, asking how I was doing and something about the weather in New York. He was curious if I'd already dropped Zoe off, and I told him I had. "Okay, please open the door," he texted. And there he was, standing with a bouquet of huge red roses. "You promised me a date," he smiled. It was February 14, Valentine's Day.

He took me out, and I'm not going to give you any details, although he told me so many times that oversharing is one of my biggest issues, but trust me

— Morris (I guess he deserves a real name now) was right. I'm afraid I'm not going to leave him anytime soon, and I can't complain. So far, it's the best relationship I've ever had.

The next morning, I got back to chasing my dream. My first order of business: finding a venue. I headed to BAM (Brooklyn Academy of Music) to discuss the space for our first run. I had been there a few years before the war, planning to bring Kirill Serebrennikov's Gogol Center to Brooklyn's top theater. However, the Gogol Center was shut down in June 2022, shortly after the war began, and I never had the chance to bring it to New York.

Naturally, when we started working on *Our Class*, BAM came to mind. The arts institution across the East River from Manhattan had produced and showcased a lot of alternative theater productions, and I felt it could be the perfect match for us. After leaving Morris that day, I texted him, saying, "I hope you bring me luck."

When I arrived at BAM, Sara and Anastasia were already there. The stage seemed perfect for us, and we had a positive meeting with the Brooklyn team before they checked the dates and said they were fully booked for the next fall and winter and, regretfully, couldn't take us. I was so upset. Sara took a train back to Boston, and I had to continue my search for a venue.

It was a real pain to find the right theater. There were many Broadway-style venues with over five hundred seats, but those were too big for us in terms of both budget and regulations. Then there were many smaller venues that seated between one hundred and two hundred people, but they were too tiny. In total, we found that there were fewer than twenty locations in all of New York City that could host an off-Broadway show with around four hundred seats, which we needed. Those venues were in high demand and booked for years in advance. We went through a lot of options and eventually settled on the Little Shubert Theatre, a beautiful spot on Theatre Row in Manhattan, about half a mile west of Broadway. The day we visited the theater in March 2023, Igor liked the stage but was concerned about having to sell tickets for 499 seats. It was International Theater Day, so I took a photo for my Instagram announcing that we were starting a new project together.

The premiere was scheduled for September 12, 2023. However, an agreement with the venue took months to finalize. We had to negotiate conditions, go back and forth, and then one of their team members went on vacation, leaving us stuck in the process. In the meantime, we started bringing the cast and other members of the creative team together. It felt like assembling a puzzle with missing pieces, with actors asking about the venue, sponsors asking about the actors, and so on.

When we began casting, we agreed that we didn't need big-name stars. Sure, stars help sell a show. Sometimes the ticket prices for well-known actors on Broadway soar to $1,000! It's outrageous and unaffordable for many people, and yet the show still sells out. Our ticket prices were meant to be ten times lower. But it wasn't the reason why we decided to go without one big star in the cast. What was even more important was that all the actors were on equal footing; we needed a strong ensemble, not a star with a bunch of supporting actors.

Igor had initially envisioned each actor playing a character at the age they died. For example, Abram, played by Richard Topol, was the first actor we confirmed, since he was the oldest character in the story. We found Richard through Jessica Hecht, a well-known American actress who had worked with Igor on another project. It turned out to be a perfect fit.

I insisted we work with the talented Russian actor Andrey Burkovskiy. He was my friend, but I also had immense respect for him. Born in a Siberian town, Andrey fell in love with theater at a young age and dreamed of becoming an actor. He went on to graduate from the prestigious Moscow Art Theatre School, the alma mater of the world-renowned Stanislavski method. Over the years, Andrey built a successful international career on stage and in film, performing at the iconic Moscow Art Theatre and starring in award-winning films.

When the war broke out, Andrey left Russia with his wife and two children. They first relocated to Israel, then, a year later, to the States. He did not give any interviews about it; he simply and quietly began rebuilding his career from scratch, learning English and taking part in a very small production.

In Russia, Andrey was a huge star. He was in all the hit TV shows and movies, had lead roles at the Moscow Art Theater, and even played hockey with an amateur team that Putin would occasionally show up to.

One time, someone from our cast asked me how famous Andrey was back home, and I said, "He's pretty much the Russian Brad Pitt." It was meant as a joke, and Andrey hated it — he didn't think it was accurate at all. But of course, once it was out there, it totally stuck. After that, actors wouldn't stop calling him "our Russian Brad Pitt," much to his dismay.

My point is, Andrey would have been far more financially successful if he had stayed, but he chose to leave.

After two and a half years in the United States, Andrey and I launched an acting studio, Seagull NYC, based on the Stanislavski method, as a tribute to his alma mater here in New York. After we announced the opening of our studio, major Russian newspapers reported, saying, "Burkovskiy stole one of Russia's greatest secrets — the Stanislavsky method — and is selling it in America." But the acting studio came much later. Back in 2023, I had to convince Sara that Andrey would be perfect for *Our Class*. Her concern was the weakness of his English, but I was confident that his dedication would make the accent a non-issue. Igor was on my side and even built Andrey's character, Menachem, around that unique aspect. Andrey quickly became one of the most popular actors in our production, especially with the audience.

Once Andrey joined the team, he immediately suggested Stephen Ochsner — another excellent choice. Stephen is an American actor from a small town in Colorado who, fifteen years ago, fell in love with Russia. He moved there to study language and theater, achieving a great deal and becoming a successful actor in Moscow. His Russian is so fluent that both Russians and Americans considered him one of their own. Stephen returned to the U.S. in 2022. When we reached out to him with the offer, he jumped into our project right away. He looked like his Jewish character, Jakub Katz. For the rest of the cast, we turned to casting directors, and Sara was in charge of this tricky process.

In the spring, we moved on to finding a set designer — someone who could bring the scenery to life on stage. Igor had long dreamed of working with Jan Pappelbaum, an outstanding set designer primarily associated with the Schaubühne theater in Berlin. During one of our planning sessions, Igor mentioned Jan's name again, and our project designer Eric Dunlap, who worked with him before, suggested, "Why not try writing to him?" I've always been someone who believes in asking, so I agreed, saying, "Why not?" Eric then sent Jan an email introducing Igor, and to our surprise, he responded.

Igor set up a Zoom with Jan, and later we learned that he had never had such an interesting artistic conversation in his life. Jan was in! Shortly thereafter, Jan laid out the entire concept for the set design. Jan envisioned the set as a wall resembling a massive blackboard. We discussed setting the play in a school, and he proposed using the board and chalk not only as the setting but also as a tool for storytelling — transforming the narrative into one big history lesson through writing on the board. The audience would witness the written and erased histories, names, and narratives. A well-known figure in the world of set design, Jan brought his expertise and vision to life in our project, and we felt incredibly fortunate to collaborate with him. What's more, we were very grateful that he agreed to work for a reasonable fee.

In May 2023, we rented a venue in downtown Manhattan and arranged the first meeting with the whole cast to do a full reading of the script. It was exciting because for the first time, we'd get a taste of the sheer emotional power of the play. The cast had read the script beforehand, of course, but could not imagine what it would be like in this first reading. At that point, we hadn't fully cast all the roles, and Igor asked the actors, who were gathered together in a circle made of chairs, to read the play. Meanwhile, Richard and Stephen were present on Zoom, which is how the idea of using a TV later in the production came about.

It was a revelation for me because I had never heard the play read out loud in English. I had read it and watched it many times in Russian, but reading it on paper was one thing — hearing it spoken was completely different. When the crucial rape scene began, I started crying. The actors hadn't even begun performing yet, but it all came alive in front of me. There was a moment when they paused. I guess it was unusual for them to see the executive producer in such a vulnerable state. My daughter Anastasia was sitting there as well and texted me, "Mom, it's embarrassing. You know how it's going to end. Can you stop crying, please?" It just had a truly personal weight for me. It was the second time since the war began that I had cried like a baby, and I couldn't help myself.

Strong emotions affected others on the project too. On July 10, the anniversary of the massacre in the town of Jedwabne, Igor, Sara, and Jan traveled to Poland to meet the playwright Tadeusz Slobodzynek and visit places tied to the events and setting of the play, including Auschwitz.

It had a huge impact on Igor. The impressions from this trip, in a way, shaped his artistic approach and his direction of *Our Class*. Later, he shared that the most unexpected thing was how quiet it was in Jedwabne, with only a single monument to show what horror had happened there. He found that no one wanted to talk about it. Even the church was closed on the day, the official anniversary of the massacre, and Igor wasn't able to go inside. It seemed that Jedwabne was keeping its terrible past buried.

We were still trying to deal with our potential venue when one day Sara received a strange email from the Under the Radar festival. Someone on their team asked when she could send over promotional materials for *Our Class*. Confused, Sara immediately called the festival director to find out what was going on. He simply said, "You can consider this an official invitation." When Sara called me, she was nearly screaming with excitement. Under the Radar is one of the most renowned festivals for experimental theater in New York, so being part of such a prestigious festival was a huge opportunity for us.

Sara was using every opportunity she had to convince everyone to hear more about *Our Class*, so of course, she told the Under the Radar director Mark Russell about our upcoming premiere. At first, though, he didn't express any interest in it.

Who knows what really happened or why the universe decided to be kind to us? Maybe it was impressed by Sara's dedication, or perhaps Russell suddenly awakened to what our project was about, or maybe BAM had a last-minute cancellation. It also could have helped that BAM and the Under the Radar festival were closely connected. BAM serves as a major partner and hosts one of the festival's programs. Obviously, they trusted Russell's judgment, as he is one of the major players in the theater industry.

What matters is the outcome: our victory. They gave us a four-week run in January 2024. And just for the record, Morris still insists it happened because he brought me luck — after all, I took a tour of BAM right after our first date.

With the schedule pushed back to January, rehearsals were now set to begin in December. The system in New York is completely different from what I was used to. In Russian theater, directors often have three months — sometimes even six — for rehearsals, as theaters typically have their own rehearsal spaces, and the cast is on the payroll. But in New York, we didn't have a dedicated rehearsal studio, and when you rent one, you only get four weeks to rehearse. That makes it feel like an impossible mission, especially when you're working with ten actors on a three-hour play, including one intermission.

As producers, we were worried that when we would start rehearsals, our actors wouldn't know each other yet, and we'd lose valuable time just on the getting-to-know-each-other process.

So Sara came up with a plan. She suggested that we should all meet earlier and build a sense of trust and begin steeping ourselves in the play. So in November, we organized an offsite meeting, with Sara inviting the whole team to her family house in Berkshire, Massachusetts. It was like a getaway resort. Berkshire was famous for summer theater and dance festivals, surrounded by the beauty of golden autumn and local farmers markets.

According to the union contract, we couldn't arrange a rehearsal or any work-related meeting, so we simply invited everyone to this wonderful place for some fun, dinner, and games. It was completely optional, but everyone showed up. On the first night, we had a lovely dinner. I cooked Russian dumplings, and Sara made her signature salad. Almost fifteen of us spent the entire weekend together. Besides the actors, we also brought our composer, Anna Drubich, from California, and our dramaturg and scholar, Dr. Rachel Merrill Moss, whose research focused on Jewish performances in Poland. She gave us a history lesson of sorts and we shared the video from Poland that the team had shot while they were there.

We ate, drank, talked, and sang songs — just what good friends do. Sara and I shared a bit about ourselves, and each of the members spoke about themselves, followed by one personal thing about how the play resonated with them. One cast member, Gus Birney, who played Dora — the Jewish girl burned in the barn and raped by her classmates — is an experienced actress, but without formal education. She dropped out of school in the ninth grade, so much of the context around the Holocaust was unfamiliar to her. At one point, amid our emotional discussions, she almost started crying. I remember her saying something like, "Guys, when I signed up for this project, I read the play, but I didn't realize how important this was. It was just a job, but now I understand — it's much more, it's really important."

By the end of the offsite, we felt like a family. We shared photos on our official *Our Class* page to start promoting the play, and all the actors began reposting them. After that, I knew we had reached a new level of intimacy. I couldn't wait to see what would come of this newfound artistic chemistry.

Chapter 11

The contract with BAM was arranged by December, so we were able to start rehearsing. The premiere was set for January 12.

By that time, aside from the cast, we had finalized the music and costumes, I invited the composer Anna Drubich, who I had always wanted to work with. I followed her works for many years and knew that she was the right person to work on the moving material of *Our Class*.

The daughter of legendary Russian director Sergei Solovyov and one of the most beautiful Russian actresses, Tatyana Drubich, Anna inherited a world where beauty and artistry were simply a part of life, so I had a feeling that she would perfectly capture the emotional heart of the play.

I reached out to Anna, who lived in Los Angeles for many years, and she immediately agreed to join us. After I shared the concept of the play with her, she worked closely with Igor. They had calls to discuss scenes, and she'd create reference tracks. Each scene had its own musical theme, and much of the music evolved during the rehearsal process.

Another talent I was fortunate to bring on board was our costume designer, Sasha Ageeva. We wanted to capture the essence of each character while keeping them relatable to the audience — something grounded in reality, not too theatrical. Initially, we worked with a New York costume designer, but after three attempts of going back and forth and receiving her sketches, nothing quite fit.

By the third attempt, I finally told Igor, "Okay, this isn't working. We have to stop wasting our time." But it wasn't as simple as I thought, because based on the contract, we had to pay the designer in full, even though she hadn't delivered what we needed. It was mid-November, we didn't have a designer that we wanted to work with, and we were running low on money. The only thing we had was a clear vision. We already knew exactly what kind of costumes we needed, so I told Sara, "Give me two days, and I'll find a new designer."

I reached out to my contacts for recommendations, and that's how we found Sasha, a designer based in Serbia who left Russia when the war began. I was driving to Washington, D.C. with my friend when someone shared her phone number with me. After exchanging a few messages, I asked her to jump on a call. We spoke for almost an hour, and from the first minute, I knew she was the one. She finished sentences I started, understood every reference, and immediately responded with creative ideas that were on point.

Sasha asked for half the price we'd been paying and requested three days to deliver sketches. Those first designs perfectly aligned with our vision. We were on the clock now and had to hire an assistant in New York to work closely under her guidance. With no time to produce costumes, the assistant ran around the city to find the materials our designer requested. Sasha is an absolute gem, and she has collaborated with Igor on three other projects already.

We also needed a makeup artist and hair stylist but didn't have money to hire someone to create all the images and then help them get ready every night. So I came up with an idea.

I had a friend. Timur was a very well-known hair artist in Russia. Timur had worked for many fashion magazines, shows and fashion brands in Moscow, but as an LGBTQ+ person, they eventually began facing challenges at work and ended up fleeing Russia a few years before the war started.

Here in New York, Timur was figuring things out — working nights helping local drag queens with hair, working days at a small hair salon, and spending time with a bunch of friends, building a new life. I love Timur. I trust them completely — I only let them touch my hair.

So I called them and said, "Listen, do you want to work off Broadway?" And they said, "Are you kidding me? It's always been my dream!" I said, "Can you come up with something simple — a style for ten actors that they can do by themselves every night for four weeks?" Timur said, "Definitely." And that's how our show's style was born.

Next, we faced a dramatic twist in our off-Broadway journey — at least for me: the actors' union. By December, rehearsals were in full swing. One of the biggest expenses from our budget — and one I hadn't anticipated as a newly minted producer in New York — was dealing with the labor union.

Coming from Moscow, where no similar unions exist, the process was foreign to me. In Russia, producing a new play was straightforward: You negotiated directly with the actors, agreed on payment, and paid them. But in the United States, it was a different story. Once you cast your actors, you were not allowed to pay them directly or with different contracts. If you needed additional actors, you couldn't simply bring someone you knew or someone you thought would be perfect for the role — you had to inform the union and arrange the open call. That means an additional cost for you as a producer. Most major venues — including Broadway and off-Broadway productions — require actors to be union members and comply with union regulations. This means that after speaking with an actor, you first have to contact their agent. If the agent accepts your offer, you then sign the contract with the union. The catch? Many agents have little interest in off-Broadway productions, as their commission is relatively small. I know of one case where an agent deliberately ignored a producer's calls and emails, hoping to keep their actor available for a potential and more lucrative commercial gig. Sadly, the actor lost out on the theater role. In such situations, even if an actor is perfect for the part, you often have to move on to another candidate — no one wants to waste time. There are many professional agents in this industry, but they are busy and not really looking for young off-Broadway actors to work with.

The most challenging part of dealing with the union is that you need all your offers accepted before you can finalize the deal with the union itself. In our case, we had a cast of ten actors, three understudies, a stage manager, and an assistant stage manager. You can imagine how complex it was. Once the union approved us, we had to pay a bond of nearly $50,000. This money is typically refunded after the show closes — provided there are no issues or additional payments. In my case, it took six months to get our bond back.

Truth is, a lot of people in the industry complain about the union and how damaging some of its rules are for theater — but only in whispers. It's like having a big, unpleasant neighbor watching your every move. You don't want to cross them because they have the power to destroy you.

Ironically, I'm now a union producer myself. Ridiculously, my company is classified under a Tier 5 contract, which technically makes us more "successful" (and thus subject to stricter rules and higher pay scales) than some of New York's oldest experimental theaters. It was my first off-Broadway production, we were a nonprofit staging in a tiny venue with limited seating, which meant no one was walking away with any profit, and still we have to pay more and follow more rules. This is how complicated the situation in this field is right now. I had to learn the hard way — feeling as though I was constantly battling a massive, merciless machine that seemed determined to crush our artistic vision, rather than support it.

The union sets minimum wages, even when actors would gladly work for less. While I fully support fair pay, the lack of direct communication makes everything painfully complicated and time consuming. The contract we signed outlined the actors' wages, working conditions, benefits, and other union protections. It also made the kind of rehearsal model we were accustomed to in Russia — where directors might spend three months rehearsing in the venue — impossible. The economics in the United States. simply didn't allow for it. You couldn't afford to hire actors for that long, which meant you were forced to keep rehearsal periods as short as possible. Working with the union also came with its share of absurd challenges. For instance, sometimes I wanted to meet with the actors before the scheduled rehearsal to discuss creative ideas. The actors were eager to come, knowing it would benefit the play. But the union could block the meeting if the actors hadn't been given the required break hours between rehearsals — or worse, they could charge us overtime for holding it.

Even during rehearsals, we were required to have ten-minute breaks. During those breaks, the director wasn't allowed to approach the actors with notes or feedback, as the contract mandated they "rest." Some actors took this seriously; others were more flexible. The most frustrating part? Some actors would report you to the union if they caught you speaking with them — even if they themselves wanted to talk.

And then there were the specialist requirements. If your play included a rape scene, you were required to hire a violence and intimacy specialist and provide documentation proving their presence. If there were weapons in the play, you needed a weapons specialist on-site. On paper, these rules seem reasonable — even useful — but in practice, they can suffocate the magic of theater. For example, union stage managers were required at every rehearsal, but if you wanted to divide your group by, say, acting rehearsal in one room and movement in another, you would expect the choreographer to work with the dancers while the director worked with the cast. But according to the rules, you couldn't do that and would have to wait until the union stage manager or their assistant joined. Yet often, only the dancer and choreographer were truly needed in the room.

In *Our Class*, we had an incredibly emotional and heavy rape scene. Staging it was excruciating for everyone — the actress, the actors playing the perpetrators, and the director. During such moments, the creative process is fragile and raw. The director carefully maps out the scene, discussing it with the team: "Let's try it this way." The actors step into position — one climbing a stepladder, others moving into place. Every detail is considered. Meanwhile, in the audience for the rehearsal, a violence specialist sits and observes. I sat there too, barely daring to breathe, completely immersed in the creative process. At that moment, something brilliant — maybe even genius — was being born. You don't dare sneeze. You don't check your phone. You're entirely present, witnessing the raw alchemy of theater.

The scene is unfolding. The actress is fully immersed in her performance, delivering her lines with intensity. She's in the middle of it, and the director doesn't interrupt. Then, suddenly, the intimacy specialist's voice cuts through: "Sorry, are you feeling comfortable? How comfortable do you feel?" Believe it or not, this kind of thing happens constantly. And when you're in a long rehearsal, it becomes exhausting. My nerves just can't take it. Here's the point that I want to emphasize: I am not against the rules, I just want to point out that some people could use these rules and take advantage. In our case, we had to let one of the actors go because he appeared to exploit every loophole and created tension for the entire team.

For example, one day, the actors were throwing small bags filled with powder — a key moment in a murder sequence where characters toss the bag. He would interrupt scenes, pause constantly, and ask questions — even during the intense bag-throwing moment — like, "How many times do you think I should throw it?" I thought, I don't know, as many times as it takes to get it right?

Then he'd add comments like, "What if my shoulder starts hurting from throwing this? I already feel something. What do we do then?" I had no words for that. I felt he just knew how to abuse the system, and each interruption shattered the collective momentum.

At some point, he just stopped, turned to me, and said, "As a producer, our safety and health are your main priority, right?" I wanted to say everything I was thinking, but decided against it, as I knew he was just trying to escalate the situation. I met people like him before; they all act the same regardless of language or nationality. I just nodded and left the room.

A few actors in the cast told me later that they were annoyed by his attitude, but as union members they couldn't say anything. One sent me a private message saying, "Sofia, I respect you very much, I am sorry your job is so hard." That meant a lot to me.

But, yes, as if it needs to be said, as a producer, I want to confirm that safety and health are my main priorities as well as creating a talented art masterpiece during this process.

The other actors continued without issue, but this one bad apple seemed inclined to do everything in his power to sabotage the process without outright saying, "I don't want to do this." It wasn't just me who was frustrated with him — Igor and Sara agreed that he was a disaster, but what could we do? We did, however, find a solution. Under the union contract, if the three of us agreed that an actor wasn't right for a role, we could let him go, but it had to be done before the first performance. We still had to pay him, but that's what we did.

And again, I want to say something important. I may not have known the rules, but sometimes it takes an outsider to see what insiders no longer notice. When you're too close to something, you can become blind to its flaws. Even if I haven't described everything perfectly, I believe I've identified real challenges facing the unions today.

My goal isn't to criticize for the sake of criticism — it's to help make things better. Because I'm not going anywhere this time. One day, I would like to open a small repertoire theater in New York, where creativity is free and not restricted by politics. But with all the complex union rules today, I'm not sure if this dream could ever become reality. The challenges are serious, and finding a way through them feels uncertain. Right now, it's only a dream — one I'm still a little afraid to believe in.

Anyway, let's go back. We quickly found not just a replacement, but a brilliant actor who made the role deeper and stronger. As I've said before, everything happens for a reason.

I was impressed by how patiently Igor handled the situation. I also began to admire his way of working with actors and achieving the virtuosic balance between two worlds: Russian and American theater. *The New York Times* called him "artistically ambitious" and one of the most inventive directors working in the United States. Aside from that, Igor is a genuinely good person who truly cares about his work and knows how to keep his composure during tough moments like that one.

Our marketing team was working hard as well, barely sleeping as we kept piling on task after task. Two of the key players were our designer, Gosha Chubukin, and our marketing manager, Anya Rylnikova, who were based in Israel. When I moved to New York, they relocated to Tel Aviv from Moscow. They've been with me for years. Anya joined right out of university, and now she's an absolute pro. Gosha is one of the most talented graphic artists I've ever worked with — his way of thinking has always fascinated me. We've done so many amazing projects together — even the cover of this book was designed by him. When we started working on *Our Class*, I immediately told Sara that I couldn't do it without Gosha and Anya. I trusted them completely, knowing that I could count on their vision, creativity, and instincts.

When we were brainstorming for *Our Class*, we spent a ton of time figuring out the concept. We were determined to move away from the usual, cliché school imagery. I'll never forget one particular Zoom call a few days after the Hamas terrorist attacks of October 7, the day another "war" began when Hamas terrorists took hostages from Israel. It was a usual call when suddenly, in the middle of our meeting, rockets started flying in Israel. The alarms went off in Tel Aviv, and Gosha and Anya just said, totally calmly, "We need to go to a safe room right now." That is the Israeli phrase for "bomb shelter." It was surreal. What made it even more intense was that, just before, Gosha had come up with the matchbox barn-house concept, inspired by the war in Ukraine. And now, here he was, sitting in a bomb shelter — making the whole thing feel even more raw and real. Later, we ended up using Gosha's design on bags and other merchandise. It became more than just a visual — it turned into a symbol of everything we'd been through together.

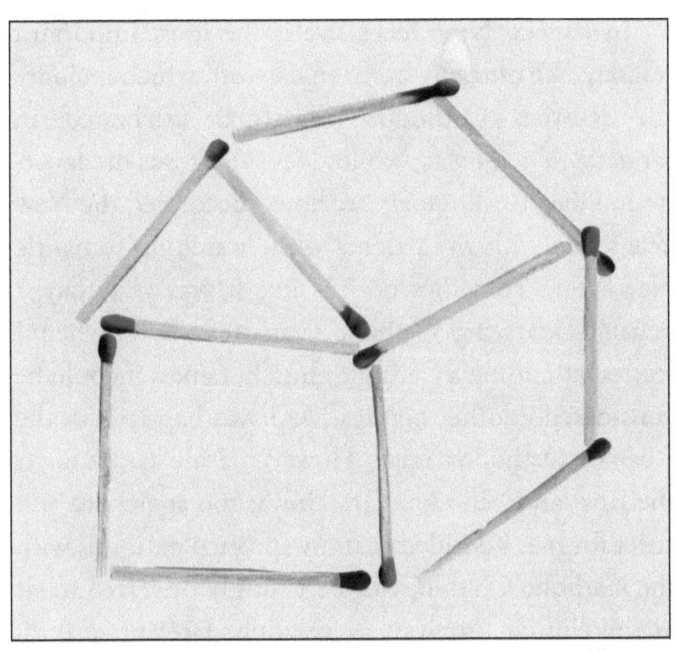

Image created by Gosha Chubukin

Chapter 12

Finally, it was Christmas and family time for all.

In Russia, New Year's Eve is the most important holiday. We officially have ten days off, which includes the Russian Orthodox Christmas celebrated in January. When I was a child, New Year's was my favorite holiday. I still remember how I decorated the New Year's tree with my parents while watching romantic New Year's comedies on TV like it was yesterday. I began celebrating Catholic Christmas later, when I started attending a Catholic church. I guess it could be considered another betrayal, as I was baptized in the Russian Orthodox faith. However, I always thought the Russian Orthodox Church was too aggressive and strict for me. I decided that my spiritual path was with the Catholic Church. Maybe I simply preferred to sit at the church. Anyway, as an adult, I celebrate both December 25, Catholic Christmas (usually attending church services with my kids), and New Year's Eve. A year ago, when I was feeling depressed, it was the first time I didn't take Zoe to church on Christmas Eve, and we didn't celebrate New Year's. We simply went to bed at 9:00 p.m.

That New Year felt different. I finally sold my huge five-bedroom apartment in Moscow and bought a small but beautiful two-bedroom apartment in Manhattan. My American friends said that I should rent instead, but for me, the concept of having my own home after all those months of uncertainty was so important that I couldn't help myself. The apartment was renovated, so I moved in immediately. The first thing I did was buy a tiny pup for Zoe, who, since the beginning of the war, had been missing our dog, whom we'd left behind with my sister in Russia. We named her Cookie, which was the pet name Morris called me. And I bought my Christmas tree. Some Russians in America skip buying Christmas trees because they've noticed that Americans just toss them out the day after Christmas. So they grab a free tree off the street and take it home to celebrate the New Year!

That Christmas, Morris, Zoe, and I spent time together. It was our first family trip, and I was a bit nervous at first, but everything turned out great. Perhaps it was because the real Santa Claus was traveling with us! Zoe's seat on the plane was next to a kind elderly man with a long white beard and Santa's hat who mentioned he was heading to the Caribbean for work, as he had a Santa duty there. All the kids on the plane were taking pictures with him, and so did we. However, Zoe was a bit skeptical and kept insisting that he wasn't the real Santa. Despite that, it was a wonderful trip, and Zoe got along really well with Morris.

After that trip, she started introducing him as her stepdad when he would drop her off at school or at playdates. At home, she called him Momo, saying, "I have my Mama and my Momo." After Christmas, Morris had to travel for business, so we celebrated New Year's without him at my place.

To step into 2024, I invited my new friends, our actors, Andrey Burkovskiy and Stephen Ochsner, and their families. We agreed to have an early dinner at my place around 5:00 p.m. Moscow was seven hours ahead of New York, and we all had friends or family there, so we decided to celebrate the Russian New Year since it was already midnight in Moscow. After that, we planned to take the kids ice skating at Central Park.

The table was a feast of famous Russian dishes including olivier salad, beet salad, red caviar, and herring under a fur coat. The whole day I cooked with my daughter Anastasia, amd my mom would have been proud of our culinary masterpieces. We lit candles on the table, symbolizing warmth and hope. I felt happy and truly cherished the joyful moment. We were laughing and enjoying the music when my eldest daughter said, "It's already midnight in Moscow. We need to make a wish now." As a child, she used to do this every New Year as an old Russian tradition: While the chimes on the historic Kremlin tower strike twelve times, you write your wish on a piece of paper, burn it, drop the ashes into a glass of champagne, and drink it. If you managed to do it while the chimes were still ringing, your wish would come true. This time, Anastasia suggested we do it together.

Andrey raised his glass and said, "I wish for all your dreams to come true in your new place, that you're happy, that everything works out. I wish for everything to come true, for everything to ignite for you here. You are in blossom here, I look at you and you are burning with ideas again, you are like a fire, just keep going, don't stop!"

We clinked our glasses, and at that exact moment... my daughter screamed, "Mom, you're on fire!" The jacket I was wearing had brushed against the candle, and it flared up. At exactly midnight in Moscow, my past life was indeed quite literally burning away. My jacket had caught fire!

We quickly poured a glass of water on my jacket, and the disaster was averted. Everything turned out fine, but we did mark the occasion with a video: New Year's footage of me with my jacket on fire.

Morris called me a few minutes later. No matter how far away he was, he always found a way to be with us — even if only by phone. When I told him about the incident, he said, "You see? As someone who sees signs in everything, you should take this as a clear one: Your Moscow life is officially over." I nodded, but strangely, I didn't feel sadness. When I called my mom to wish her a happy New Year, I told her that next year would be incredibly significant for me, and I hoped we would find a way to be together. She simply replied, "I want you to be happy and feel loved." And in that moment, I felt a deep sense of peace and harmony, knowing that her love, no matter the distance, would always guide and protect me.

Chapter 13

One week before the premiere at BAM, we were almost ready — ten actors and two understudies, as required by the union's rules. Then, suddenly, one of the actors tested positive for Covid-19. According to BAM's guidelines in January 2024, anyone who tested positive had to wait five days before returning to the stage.

Everyone was vaccinated, of course, but we had to replace that actor. And then, a second actor tested positive. At that point, we no longer had a male replacement. Normally, the protocol would dictate rescheduling the premiere.

But I had poured so much into making this happen — securing sponsors, organizing every vendor for the after-party, and coordinating with people flying in from the United Kingdom, Israel, and other places. This premiere was a huge deal for us, and canceling just wasn't an option for me.

The rest of the team was seriously considering calling off the premiere. Sara was trying to soften the blow, saying it wasn't the worst thing — we could reschedule. But during a WhatsApp group call, I made it clear: Canceling is not an option. What can we do?

At the time, we felt we had only about thirty minutes to come up with a solution.

That's when Sara said, "Igor, what about Ben?"

"Who is Ben?" I asked.

She was referring to an actor named Benjamin Evett from Boston who had worked with Sara and Igor on other productions. We needed someone who could step into the absent role seamlessly, who knew Igor's direction and whom they could trust. So we agreed to ask him. Igor said, "If we send him the script and get him into rehearsal now, he can train on the three-hour train ride and head straight to the theater. I can guide him on the phone first."

I said, "Amazing! Do you think he can learn long monologues that quickly?"

Igor came up with a brilliant idea that Ben could act holding the script. It turned out Ben was a masterful memorizer and barely needed it.

I didn't want to reschedule the premiere because I felt responsible to everyone who had committed to making *Our Class* happen. I was managing the press, inviting celebrities, and working closely with sponsors I'd invited to the show and the after-party.

It wasn't so easy to find partners for our dramatic play. The truth was, people were much more inclined to support Broadway shows and events like Fashion Week. I did not have a reputation or a famous name in New York yet, so in order to make a difference at this critical moment in my career, I reached out to my network.

One day a friend sent me the number of some-one called Mohamed. I'd been told that he had just launched a champagne brand and might be interested in providing bottles for the event.

So I texted him — "Hey, Mohamed, I got your number from a friend. My name is Sofia, I'm a pro-ducer, and we've got an off-Broadway show coming up in New York. I was wondering if you would be inter-ested in supporting our premiere." I attached the pre-sentation deck. I didn't even know who he was. I sent so many messages like that, and honestly, most of them just sat on my phone with no response. So when he immediately replied, I was really surprised. He said he was in Singapore, busy traveling, but he took a quick look at what we were working on and asked if I could jump on Zoom right away. "Of course," I replied.

The first thing I saw was a sweet Black kid running around in front of the screen. Mohamed jumped in after a few seconds saying that he needed to put his son to sleep but that he was happy to hear me out. He was Black, liv-ing in Singapore, and named Mohamed — what could he possibly have in common with *Our Class*?

I told him our story, my story, and without hesi-tation, he said, "Sofia, It's crazy, but the story of your play is so relevant to me that I want to support you as much as I can. My story is also sort of crazy, as I might be the only Black person with the name Mohammed who is actually Jewish." That's how we ended up with champagne for our premiere and how Mohamed and I became friends. You never know how and where you will find partners and supporters.

Since we were such an international project, I wanted to reflect that in our food menu. There was a restaurant in Manhattan, Mari Vanna, known for its Russian-Ukrainian cuisine. I reached out to see if they'd be interested in partnering with us to create something special for the premiere. After a series of meetings, fine-tuning the menu, and discussing how everything would look, we came up with something amazing.

Mari Vanna was the restaurant where I invited Igor and Sara after we signed the contract with BAM. I am a huge fan of their food. They have the best roasted potatoes with mushrooms, delicious dumplings, and my favorite pickles. Part of my Russian DNA is to have a feast for any special occasion. In addition, this restaurant has this tradition where you can write what you want on their wallpaper, and so I wrote "Our Class NYC 2023" on that contract-signing day as a manifestation of our future success. It became a special place for us. Fun fact: We used to have Mari Vanna back in

Russia, but I was never a fan. I also didn't really like Russian food. But now, I'm obsessed.

When the big day arrived of the premiere, Mari Vanna delivered everything exactly as planned. By that point, rescheduling felt completely out of the question, not just because postponing would've cost money but also because of the effort and dedication they'd poured into making it perfect. Letting down my partners wasn't an option.

Chapter 14

We premiered on January 12, 2024 at BAM, and my precious dream had come true. Not only had I produced my first show in New York, but it was the one I dearly wanted it to be. Ben, the replacement actor, was amazing, and no one outside our team noticed anything. We paid him for two weeks, and he covered the first weekend of performances before our original actor came back with a negative Covid result. Sometimes, you just have to be creative and determined. I don't like giving up easily. I've found there's often a solution if you look hard enough for it.

The rest of the cast was incredible on stage. The first performance is always the most difficult one, but they managed to handle the stress and did a beautiful job. The acting was deep, thoughtful, emotional, and magical. Long standing ovations after that first show proved my point. I was happy the show was strong, and I felt relieved. I remember telling myself, "Good job, Sofia!"

To I don't really like premieres. It's probably an unusual statement, considering that I'm an executive producer, but premieres always bring additional stress and put a lot of pressure on me.

This pressure ruins my mood and I simply cannot enjoy the creative side of the experience. VIP guest seating is the worst — there's always someone who can't come, and you end up with empty seats because you were expecting them. It's painful, and I take it very personally.

The next reason to freak out is the press. There are always bad reviews, always someone who doesn't like the show. As we know, "A great review is great. A bad review is the worst." Honestly, I get it; so many times I went to a show that I didn't produce, and I loved it, but critics didn't get it at all. What's more, I often find that the majority of contemporary productions that I don't like, the press rave about. I am okay with bad reviews, it's better than nothing, but the actors, directors, and choreographers are so fragile and these reviews hurt them badly. A single devastating review can crush a run.

My favorite part of my job is the creative process, rehearsals, work in progress with the team, and the end of a regular show when the audience is happy and satisfied, giving standing ovations and thanking me as a producer.

It was a great joy for me to see almost all my friends come to the BAM premiere to show their support in the cold winter month of January. They came from London, Paris, Milan, Tel Aviv, Washington, L.A.; a few even came from Manhattan. It was a big deal for busy people in January, if you know what I mean. I was so happy to be able to share this day with them, simply hug them, and thank them for coming. Unfortunately, neither my friend from Moscow nor my mom could come, but Morris was there. I was so busy hustling that I only had a chance to introduce him to Rodnyansky, but I saw him in my mind's eye, standing in a corner, smiling and drinking wine, talking to people. I felt love for him from a distance, knowing in my heart that he was there for me.

Some of our sponsors came to the premiere, most importantly, Jan Koum. Without his support, the project could not have happened. He was the first who agreed to support us, and I am forever grateful for his trust and generosity. Jan loved our play so much that he stayed for the after-party, chatting with the cast and the team, and he invited his friends later to see the show. For me, as a producer, it was important to collaborate with people who not just donate money but who show the kind of total support that Jan did. I was so pleased to see that this project was also meaningful to him. It wasn't just about money, it was much more than that. Jan immigrated to America as a kid from Ukraine. He is Jewish and his story is reminiscent of the family story of our Jewish director who came to America from Kyiv.

It's crucial to thank the people who helped you to be successful. if you get caught up in the idea that everything worked out in that exact moment, you miss the point. The moment of success is just one step, not the whole journey. That feeling of success is energy itself — it should fuel you to move forward. If you focus too much on the success — on praising yourself, celebrating — you'll lose that energy and won't push toward the next stage, the next opportunity. At least, that's how it feels to me. So I always try to thank everyone who made it possible. It's like being a mom: When your kids do something great, you want to praise them and see the positive results of that praise.

When I gave my speech, I thanked all my supporters, partners, friends, and Sara, my new partner in crime, who even ordered special hoodies for both of us with the title "Executive Producer" on the back. I told her that it had been a privilege to work with her, and this journey was just the beginning of something big and beautiful.

Closer to midnight, we got an email with a link. *The Wall Street Journal* was going to run a review in print the next morning. Everyone was excited and overwhelmed with that news.

I booked a hotel near BAM in Brooklyn, since I was practically living at the theater. We had a morning meeting, followed by rehearsals and a show at night, and I didn't have time to go home. Morris stayed with me. The next day he woke up early to go for his usual walk, while I prepared for another big day. I stepped out an hour later, and everyone at the hotel was congratulating me on my premiere. I'm thinking, okay, this is weird. I mean, the hotel bellboy even mentioned what a great review we got. Then I spotted a stack of *Wall Street Journal* newspapers at the reception. I could hardly believe it, but one whole page was dedicated to our show, and the review itself was a riveting rave. I was happy, of course, but at the same time, I was completely baffled by all this attention. Feeling paranoid, I asked the concierge, "How do all these people know about our show?" He replied, "Oh, Morris bought the newspapers and gave them to everyone this morning." I blushed, and in a fit of pique, called him, frustrated and furious: "What's wrong with you? Are you an idiot? Why are you embarrassing me here?" Probably his first thought after my outburst was a puzzled "WTF!" But dear Morris just replied, "Honey, what's wrong? It's great that you had this success, and now more people know about it. I am so proud of you!"

Now, months later, I can tell you that that scream-ing outburst belongs to the insecure Russian woman in me: the one who'd never gotten used to being praised, who was used to only being lectured to or criticized. That side of myself had never felt that I was actually good enough for something.

When I calmed down that morning, I realized there was something wrong, but not with Morris — with me.

Since we're still at the beginning of our romantic adventure, I don't want to sound overly sentimental or make it seem like he's some flawless hero — because he's not. But he is a hero to me. Morris was raised by a loving mother and an incredible grandmother. They've both passed away, but he still keeps their photo as the wallpaper on his iPhone. One day, he told me that he became the man he is because of them. They loved him unconditionally, always supported him, and shaped his view of women — especially moms — as some-thing sacred. Morris once said that since he deals with so many fights at work, he refuses to bring that energy home. "Trust but verify," I told him. But honestly, ever since we started seeing each other, he's treated me like a goddess — always with love, patience, and support. Morris and I were simply raised in different worlds. I'd never had such an experience in Russia's macho society, where many of us are just not accustomed to being praised. But after that moment in which Morris showed me such love and respect, I decided that had to change. Looking back, that gesture from Morris is one of my favorite memories from the *Our Class* premiere.

WHO'S WHO IN THE CAST?

GUS BIRNEY*
Dora

ANDREY BURKOVSKIY*
Menachem

JOSÉ ESPINOSA*
Rysiek

TESS GOLDWYN*
Zocha

WILL MANNING*
Heniek

DELILAH NAPIER*
Understudy

STEPHEN OCHSNER*
Jakub Katz

ALEXANDRA SILBER*
Rachelka/Marianna

RICHARD TOPOL*
Abram

ILIA VOLOK
Wladek

ELAN ZAFIR*
Zygmunt

UNDERSTUDY

For Gus Birney, Alexandra Silber, Tess Goldwyn DELILAH NAPIER*

STAGE MANAGEMENT

Production Stage Manager .... KYRA BOWIE*
Assistant Stage Manager .... ASHTON PICKERING*
Assistant Stage Manager .... KELSEY VIVIAN*
Stage Manager Alternate .... KAYLEIGH LAYMON*

*Indicates members of Actors' Equity Association

OUR CLASS contains material for adult audiences and mature themes. The production includes acts of violence, sexual assault and antisemitic language, as well as use of theatrical smoke and haze, strobe lights, and simulated gun shots. Recommended for ages 16+

Poster for *Our Class*. Classic Stage Company, September 2024

Poster for *Our Class*, September 2024

Actor Stephen Ochsner for *Our Class*. New York, 2024

Stage mock-up for *Our Class* by Jan
Pepelbaum. New York, 2023

Sofia Kapkov during the first rehearsal
of *Our Class*. December 2023

Sofia Kapkov, Tadeusz Słobodzianek, Igor Golyak, and Sara Stackhouse at BAM. January 2024

The cast of *Our Class* and Tadeusz
Słobodzianek at BAM. January 2024

Premiere of the second run of *Our Class*, September 2024

Igor Golyak near the Jedwabne Pogrom Memorial. July 2023

Chapter 15

The BAM run couldn't have been better: Ticket sales were strong, and as the run went on, more and more industry people started showing up. Word of mouth was spreading fast. I was happy with that because it was part of my marketing strategy.

One day, Sara received an email from a guy named Ty Rogers. He was coming to see the show the next day and wanted to meet the producers and the director if possible. He also shared his story.

Ty was a descendant of those who suffered in Poland in 1941; twenty-six of his cousins were killed in Jedwabne during the pogrom. He only learned about his past later in life when he was studying at university, and since then it became his life's mission to work against "the falsification of history," in which Poles denied their involvement in the massacre. In 1996, he published an op-ed in *The New York Times* called "Poles Have Yet to Face Their Postwar Past" with his revelations: "In researching my family's history," he wrote, "I learned that more than 1,600 Jews, practically the entire Jewish population of Jedwabne, my ancestors' hometown in northeastern Poland, were burned alive in a barn on July 10, 1941. This atrocity was not committed by the Germans, but by Polish townspeople."

In fact, Ty was instrumental in making *Our Class* possible. Based on his research, historian Jan Gross published his book *Neighbors*, which led to national controversies in Poland and the subsequent play written by Tadeusz Słobodzianek.

We liked Ty right away. He happened to be an interesting, educated man in his sixties, wearing a nice suit and speaking openly about those terrible life events. We asked him to stay afterwards to talk with the team.

That day, in the backroom, Ty shared his family photos and pictures from the past with the team. He welcomed our questions and I asked my friend, a talented videographer, to record the meeting. I had only two questions: "What would you have done if your ancestors had been on the other side of history? If they were the murderers would you still be talking about the past?" He paused and said, "I've never considered this."

The run was a success, sold out every night. Since the theater didn't have a café, my daughter and I sold chocolate, nuts, and water during intermission, chatting with the audience. Zoe was helping us on the weekends, and my son got accepted to college and was gone. Life was good.

Producers — some of them quite well known — began attending our show as well, and that's when the talks about moving the show to Broadway started. Suddenly, Sara and I were having Zoom meetings with influential people, discussing the possibility. BAM told us we were the first production they could remember to receive standing ovations after every single performance. And in New York, where standing ovations weren't exactly the norm, that really said something. They suggested we extend our run for two more weeks, and we agreed.

After the last show, I flew to Europe. First stop: the Holland Dance Festival. My company co-produced the first European tour of an American dance company called Gibney. Second stop: Paris. My friend from Moscow happened to be there. It was quite a success. The tour went great, and catching up with my best friend was even better. We spent two amazing days together, and before I left, she hugged me and said, "I'm so proud of you. A lot of people immigrate, but not everyone moves forward. Many stay stuck in the past and never do anything meaningful. But you? You started over from nothing and, in such a short time, built a whole new life." That stuck with me as I reconciled with my identity as an immigrant. On the flight back to New York, a guy asked about my accent. I told him, "I'm Russian, from Moscow, but I live in

New York." And for the first time, I felt like the pain and guilt were almost gone.

As soon as I came back, Sara and I began to consider bigger plans: To qualify for the Tony Awards, the production had to open on Broadway by April. And because of that timing, the fight for venues was very competitive. I didn't care about the award, but Sara and Igor did, so we were trying hard to make a transfer to Broadway. One of the venues we wanted reached out, and we felt lucky. But we had to raise a significant amount of money within a month, which was a huge challenge. Still, I knew it was too big a chance to pass up.

We worked tirelessly for about three weeks, but in the end the venue pulled out. It wasn't official, but we heard they found it too risky — having a controversial Russian producer, a Ukrainian director, and a play with Jewish themes. There was political change in the air that I did not pay much attention to but I should have. I see that now as my mistake.

Chapter 16

Some say that to make it in New York, you need to make it in Manhattan. Besides, some snobbish city types kept saying they wanted to come to see our show but they couldn't see themselves going to Brooklyn. So when we faced the fact that Broadway was off the table, we decided to hold the second run of *Our Class* in Manhattan anyway but on another off-Broadway stage.

The idea of being in Manhattan felt like a new beginning. That youthful energy, that feeling of never-ending possibility, was something I felt for years. When I was living full time in Moscow and visiting Anastasia in New York, I was consumed with the sense of a potential fresh start every time I landed at JFK Airport. In Moscow, it felt the opposite — I knew everyone, achieved what I wanted — and so there were zero surprises and nowhere to go. Also, I always felt that New York is a city that allows mistakes. And I believe that life, in fact, is made up of mistakes. You learn from them, move forward, and make mistakes again. I always felt somehow that a polished, clean Moscow was too artificial and fake, while New York is real, and like real life, it's messy, noisy, but beautiful because it is alive.

As soon as we decided to have a second run in Manhattan, we began that tricky game — chasing down a venue. Of course, nothing was available. Then one day, Sara called me and said, "There's this theater, Classic Stage Company (CSC), one of off-Broadway's oldest, located near 14th Street." Luckily for us, it was available in the fall, so we needed to schedule a Zoom with them as soon as possible.

It felt weird that I hadn't seen anything there, but Sara was adamant about how respected it was in the New York theater world. The Zoom call was productive — they seemed reasonable, interested in us, and more than that, the director had seen *Our Class* at BAM and was confident it was the perfect fit for their audience.

They made an ideal offer too: Instead of renting the venue to us, they would present us with the status of co-presenter. In that scenario, it wouldn't just be us holding the ball, we'd have strong partners helping with marketing and sales. Well, looking back, that turned out to be a second huge mistake on my part.

We'd planned the launch for fall 2024 at Classic Stage Company with a capacity of two hundred people. For context, the first round in January and February at BAM had been a huge success. We felt like we'd grown wings, like we were the conquerors of New York. The sales began in June, with the premiere set for September 12.

At the end of spring, I visited the empty theater for the first time. Oddly enough, I couldn't find the entrance, but then realized that first you had to walk through a little café to get there. The theater layout was unusual too. It was not a stereotypical theater with a stage and rows of seats facing the stage. The theater featured an intimate three-quarter thrust stage with 196 seats surrounded by beautiful brick walls. Although it sounded interesting, I sensed that it was not the right venue for us, but Igor and Sara were so happy about this experimental type of theater that I questioned my intuition. The only thing that I liked was the location — near Union Square — and I was also hoping that CSC had the solid audience base that they'd promised.

In Brooklyn, we had a lot of Russian-speaking people come out to support us — specifically Andrey Burkovskiy, who had his own following among immigrants. Many people from our circle came to see the show during those first weeks at BAM, and they were joined by American audiences, with well-known figures coming to see the show and suggesting the transfer to bigger venues — something that didn't pan out.

In Manhattan I did expect to see stronger sales from the beginning, but despite glowing reviews and positive word of mouth, we didn't see much new audience growth for the second run at CSC.

In fact, the first few days after the successful previews and our premiere were a complete disaster. Even though Sara kept insisting it was fine — she'd say, "It's great just for the fact that we're doing this" — for me, it felt like a producer's failure, where all the momentum we'd gained at BAM had somehow stalled.

Everyone was working so hard to turn things around, but nothing helped to change the sales situation.

I believe there were several reasons for this. First, the show was originally designed for a different layout, and maybe it didn't come across as effectively as it did at BAM. The stage felt even more dramatic, as it was smaller and more intimate. But that didn't necessarily work to our advantage. Take the rape scene as an example. Some people might want to distance themselves physically from the nightmarish scene, but at CSC, there were about thirty people sitting literally on the stage. Some left during the intermission, saying the visceral experience was too much for them. Second, it also seemed that many theatergoers had already seen the show in Brooklyn, which made it hard to fill the theater at CSC.

Timing also played a part in the disappointing showing. When we first started raising money for *Our Class* in 2023, I heard from some American funds: "Sofia, it's such a great dramatic story. But why now? It doesn't sound relevant." Then the Hamas attack of October 7 shifted the perspective. Suddenly, the funds focused on supporting Jewish arts showed interest in us.

To me, the war in Gaza felt deeply personal. I was on the board of the Israeli Festival and have collaborated with many Israeli choreographers. I spent my time in lockdown in Tel Aviv. With so many friends in Israel, I feel a special affinity for that country. So after October 7, I began expressing my support for my many Jewish friends in Israel on my personal Instagram page. That's when some of my American friends started texting me with messages like, "We know you just came to the U.S., and we just want to warn you to be careful about what you say on social media. You could get canceled here, and you're only at the start of your new life." I remember one time getting really pissed off and replying, "I appreciate that, but I'm Russian — I've already been canceled once, so I can handle being canceled twice."

I think that dynamic played a role in why our ticket sales stalled a year later when the majority of our audience this time were Americans. Sometimes it's convenient for people to adopt a safe stance when it comes to something as divisive as the war in Gaza to avoid any potential problems, and consequently, many people truly turned against Israel during these days.

While Americans were distancing themselves from the conflict, I was pulling my hair out in frustration. But when I spoke with others about it, I realized it was not an isolated situation and that it reflected the polarized emotional and political climate around us.

So even those who came and really liked the show didn't feel all that comfortable recommending it to their friends or talking about it at work, as the war-related topic had become too sensitive and they didn't want to hurt anyone's feelings. What's more, it was hard for us to combat this reality because we didn't have the resources to invest into marketing or pour millions into advertising. These kinds of projects were built on word-of-mouth, outreach, partnerships, and other similar levels of support. Based on our model and prediction, the play's audience should have been growing, but it wasn't. Sometimes there were just things you couldn't predict as a producer. The most painful part for me wasn't losing money but seeing actors performing in a half-empty theater.

We considered reducing the number of performances per week, but by then it was too late.

Sadly, even some new people on our own team didn't want to invite friends to the play due to the potential backlash from their colleagues or classmates. I don't hold that against them: This is a free country — you can make your own decisions based on your comfort zone.

But one thing I admire about America is that every voice matters. Freedom of expression — the ability to stand up and share your views, even if others disagree — is a core value. When people become too afraid to speak openly, it creates bigger problems, as we saw in the last election. Yes, it's important to be respectful of others' feelings. But being afraid to say anything "controversial" leads nowhere. Open dialogue, even when uncomfortable, is essential for a healthy society.

I was also expecting more from the Classic Stage Company. I was hoping they could draw some crowds, but they didn't seem eager to help. One day showed just how out of sync we were with CSC. I was seriously considering finishing the run earlier than planned, when the CSC director reached out to me, saying how happy they were with the play and the turnout we were getting. We were still one of their most successful plays, she said. That was the last straw, making it clear to me why I'd never heard of this theater before.

One day, while I was mulling over what to do next, a woman showed up at the theater in a wheelchair. She was in her seventies. Her name was Sara Miller, and she was the daughter of the real-life Abram Baker, one of our main protagonists, played by Richard Topol.

She came with her husband, a rabbi, who worked closely with Rabbi Abram Baker, and her son who flew from Israel to watch the play. Igor and Sara weren't at the theater, so I spent some time with the visitors after the show. They told me they loved it and were so grateful that they could see the story about their family in their own city and asked me to continue to preserve the legacy. Sara Miller, a native New Yorker, said she had never experienced antisemitism in her entire life until recently when she was bullied by an arrogant person in the hospital. She said it was scary now to be in the city she loved, and that she didn't feel it was safe for her grandchildren anymore. "You should tell this story to as many people as possible. People have a habit of forgetting history lessons easily."

I felt such warmth and happiness from her, and in that moment, I thought, "Well, this run was worth it if only for her family." When I told Sara about my conversation with her, she came up with a good idea: we should arrange a panel discussion with descendants of those who suffered from the 1941 pogrom in Jedwabne after one of our next shows. She added that many of those descendants had been sharing their stories to her in emails.

That was the moment when I realized what a roller coaster I'd been on from the get-go — moving to New York, starting this play, meeting the real people behind

Our Class, and finding all the ways to make it work. I couldn't sleep at night and decided to start writing a book describing my new life from the moment I decided to leave Russia. The next morning, I opened my Facebook account and saw a post from a journalist saying she wanted to kick off her career as a writer. Remember, I believe in signs. I texted her. The next day, I met my collaborator, Anastasia Chernikova, and we talked about the potential project for three hours. I liked her right away. She used to work for well-known magazines back in Russia and had the ambition of writing for large American publications when she moved to New York. That was hard, considering the competition among native speakers themselves, yet she was able to get published in all of them. She was talented and smart, and I felt comfortable sharing my story, the result of which you are seeing before your eyes right now. Those diaries I kept writing came in handy too.

Chapter 17

Halfway through the second run, I went to London to watch the preview of another play I had co-produced, partly to escape the embarrassment of seeing actors perform in a half-empty theater.

The play *What We Talk About When We Talk About Anne Frank* was a huge success. I was a fan of the script. The play was based on a Pulitzer-finalist short story written by the American writer Nathan Englander. So when the leading producer from London asked me a few months before the premiere to join the team as an associate producer, I said yes right away. It was a limited run. When I arrived, I realized that the beautiful, small Marylebone Theatre was similar to the BAM Fisher Theater, where we had our premiere. They were sold out and later received incredible reviews. It was a wild, funny, touching, darkly comic show. I saw all three previews, and during intermission, I sat and listened to what people were saying. The feedback was great.

One day, a group of friends were discussing the show, and one person said, "If you like it, you should go to New York and watch *Our Class*. It was a heart-stopping, brilliantly played and directed show." I smiled but didn't say that I was its arts hustler.

Over the next few days I received many compliments from people about the London show, with such comments as "Sofia, congratulations! After tremendous success in New York, it was a huge success here in London. You did it again!" I was happy to hear that. My ego was boosted, but I also knew that this was different from my all-in experience with *Our Class*. In contrast, I did nothing for this play's success. I was simply lucky to be invited on board by leading producer Oliver King.

At some point, I found myself near the Curzon90 cinema, where I once presented Russian movies I'd produced. As I walked past, a poster caught my eye: Francis Ford Coppola's latest film was showing. Oh my gosh, I thought, I have to see this! It was *Megalopolis*, the one he'd talked about at the party while I was depressed during those early days in New York. I rushed inside, bought a ticket, grabbed a glass of white wine, and sank into a seat.

I recalled that tumultuous time of self-doubt and self-loathing, and how that evening with Coppola — his presence, his insightful gaze, and inquisitive questions — cut through the noise. He wanted to know about Russia and my life, even though it was our first time meeting in person. He spoke of the many years he had dedicated to his dream movie and even compared New York to Rome before the fall of the empire, foreseeing a similar collapse of our megapolis.

Here I was, two and a half years after I met this legendary director, sitting at the movie theater in London filled with anticipation to watch the film of his dreams. And it was not what I had expected. Seriously, it was one of the worst of his movies.

Soon enough, people began leaving the theater and I began questioning whether Coppola had actually directed it. The film felt lacking in a cohesive plot and clear message, and I found it really karmic. I started laughing. Here I was, still overwhelmed by our weak second run of *Our Class* in Manhattan, feeling like a failure again, faking my success for people in London, and yet, a wave of inspiration and relief washed over me. If even great Francis Ford Coppola could create something like this — a flop that didn't draw numerous showings and rave reviews — who was I to mourn my own failure?

You know, the results can't always be great. That's true of even the most talented and successful people. That realization lifted me up and came exactly when I needed it. I took away something important from that movie, probably not exactly what Coppola would have imagined — that no matter what happens to your project, it's not the end of the world. Even if *Megalopolis* was a flop, Coppola keeps working, and he's still one of my heroes and one of the greatest directors of all time.

One reason I wrote this book was to show that no matter what happens, it doesn't mean you should stop or give up on your dream. And sometimes, solutions come from the most unexpected places — you just need to listen to yourself more closely. In this case, even a film I didn't like gave me more energy than any of the rational decisions I was trying to make.

I returned from my trip to London revitalized with more ideas on how to boost ticket sales for *Our Class*. We still didn't want to sell through services like TodayTix — aggregators that provided access to cheaper tickets — because it was a rip-off for producers. You lost money using them. The commission was too high, your ticket prices were too low, your box office was too small, the venue capacity was limited, and the run was too short.

So I came up with another idea.

This time I would go directly to Russian-speaking immigrants who'd recently moved to the States. So we started pushing sales on Telegram Channels, offering discounts and features like buy one, get one free. That eventually helped increase attendance, if not profits. Most important, though, we were able to attract a new crowd to the show

Morris, who transitioned from being my friend to my partner, gave me good advice. As a Black American originally from Ohio, he said, "What you're doing and thinking is all about Ukraine, Russia, or Jewish people, but I see it as also about White and Black people. I see it as about oppression — what happened here and how America has always been divided."

That perspective really opened my eyes to additional sales possibilities. I didn't want our show to be just for Russians or just for Jews; I wanted Americans to appreciate it too. So I began to send information about *Our Cass* to Black community groups.

During our second run, we saw more Black people in the audience. It probably also helped that CSC had a strong reputation and loyal followers among diverse communities. It helped us a lot.

In the meantime, Sara was working hard on group sales and special shows with special guests and post-discussions, which helped to convince audiences to buy tickets. One of the events was even more special for me than the others.

We had a guest named Yotam Polizer. Yotam was in charge of IsraAID, an Israel-based nongovernmental organization that responds to emergencies all over the world. When a disaster happens, like an earthquake in Turkey, the war in Ukraine, or a tsunami in Japan, humanitarian organizations are often the first to respond. IsraAID was not large, but it was incredibly mobile. Since everyone in his group goes through military training in Israel, they're highly qualified to provide medical help and rescue people. Sometimes, they even arrive at disaster sites before the Red Cross. So when the war began in 2022, Yotam was one of the first humanitarians to arrive in Ukraine.

I met Yotam not long after I'd first moved to New York. He had just returned from Ukraine and was raising money at an event I was attending. We chatted like old friends sharing the same sadness and grief.

So when Sara and I were tossing around names for these post-discussions, Yotam naturally came to mind. We invited him as a special guest, along with my close friend, film producer Alexander Rodnyansky, for a Q&A after one of the shows.

Rodnyansky had just come from Venice, where he was presenting his film *Of Dogs and Men*, which was set and filmed a few weeks after the Hamas took hostages. He's Ukrainian, so on one hand, he feels the support from those who back Ukraine in its war with Russia, but on the other, he was Jewish, and this war was also personal to him. He told us that Israeli artists were at greater risk of being canceled than Russian artists were two years ago, mainly because of Israel Prime Minister Benjamin Netanyahu's politics. I knew that he was right — as a producer who has been working for many years with Israeli dancers, I felt the same way.

We all agreed how inhumane cancel culture was. At the end of the post-discussion, Yotam was complimenting me about something, when Alexander added: "I've seen the play twice, and I am in awe of my friend for producing such a powerful statement. Sofia left behind a comfortable life in Moscow alone with her three children, and she dared to start anew in a place where there is no room for hypocrisy." It was so emotional that I burst into tears.

On the way home, I thought about politics and hypocrisy. I think of politics as the most dirty job. And wars are the worst. With performing arts, I'm trying to help people find their own answers to the craziness of the world. I'm grateful to have the right to produce shows that are relevant. At the same time, we need to keep in mind that so many people are traumatized and so could be hurt or feel offended by an art project. As a producer, whatever you decide, there will be consequences, and you have to be honest with yourself and with your audience. The question is how to keep it all in balance.

The gratifying moment for me is when the crowd leaves the theater asking themselves, "What can I do now? What can I do to stop the violence? What would I do if I were there in this situation?"

You could say that I am indulging in a patronizing voice right now, and maybe you are right. One thing that strongly reflects my production style is the fact that I became a mom very young, when I just turned twenty-one. I don't remember myself any differently. I treat my creative projects like kids too. My approach is a bit motherly — I worry when something goes wrong on a personal level and feel even more joy when things go well. I don't separate my personal and professional life, which might not be the best approach, but it's the only one I have. This could probably be seen as another mistake of mine.

Every time I'm involved in a project, people I work with become my temporary family. I don't always have the time to fully understand them, since it doesn't last for many years, but I still take conflicts deeply, even though on the surface, I appear calm, with great self-control and composure.

During the run, we had a serious conflict at work when one of the team members made an unfortunate decision on the job. It turned out some in the group had built up resentment toward others, and I had to manage the situation. It was a motherly yet professional discussion I had to navigate, surrounded by creative people who were deeply emotional. Building a great team around a project is one of a producer's essential skills.

When Andrey Burkovskiy celebrated his birthday at the end of the second run, he invited all the actors to his party. We taught everyone how to make toasts like Russians, and now, it's become a tradition. It's those little moments that bring us together. I remember a toast from Elon Zafir, a Canadian on our team. He said, "I never thought Canadians and Russians could be so similar." We all laughed, because honestly I don't think they are alike at all. But then he continued, "Neither of us are really liked by anyone." Everyone laughed, and I thought that he was actually right. My Morris was there too. When he raised his glass, he wished Andrey to succeed with our new project: an acting school called SeagullNYC because we deserved it. I hope Morris is right. Seagull NYC. I believe that this school has a lot of potential as it not just helps actors to upgrade their skills but helps all of us by using acting techniques to be a better version of ourselves.

Another crucial point to emphasize in my role as a producer is having a feel for the zeitgeist. A producer needs to sense the edge. I never take on something unless I feel it's going to work. It's either this or that — I just know. I trust my intuition, I feel it, and I listen to it. My decisions are based on intuition; there isn't an exact formula for me. Sometimes mistakes are made, but that's just part of the experience. Some might say my way of working has more of a dictator's touch, and maybe they're right. Maybe it's because I was raised in a macho culture, where being a boss — even as a woman — means acting like a man in power.

If you take risks, you're responsible for protecting the project and the team. At the same time, you need to give people the tools to work freely, knowing they'll make mistakes. But what if their mistakes could cost you your career? In that case, you have to be in charge. I guess it's all about balance. Even though I believe in democracy, I often end up being an authoritarian. I suppose that means I still have a lot to learn.

Chapter 18

I've always had a passion for learning, but my struggle was that I was constantly trying to be the perfect student. When I realized that I wasn't the best, I would always blame myself, thinking I wasn't good enough. I've always wanted to get another degree or study abroad, but I never took these opportunities. Instead, I've gained knowledge through hands-on work experience. Working on *Our Class* in particular taught me so much — it felt like earning a PhD in theater. Despite all the challenges, I have no regrets.

First, I've learned more than I ever expected. Producing my first off-Broadway show helped me get back on track and rediscover parts of myself I'd forgotten. It became my therapy and gave me a sense of purpose. When I started, I was in a dark place, but now, people introduce me as a producer again, not a refugee. In the beginning, I heard comments like, "Your English isn't great," or "You don't know this market," and it made me doubt myself. But now, I've found my place again, and I'm proud of what I've accomplished.

Second, I've realized that what matters most to me is working on meaningful projects that help others feel better. Money and fame are nice, but the satisfaction of creating something impactful — something that can heal — is what truly drives me. *Our Class* succeeded not because I sought success, but because I poured my own pain into it. That authenticity helped me find the resources and people to bring the project to life.

Third, *Our Class* helped heal my trauma. I'm no longer afraid to embrace my Russian identity. I've started reading and writing in Russian again, and I'm actively making sure my daughter, Zoe, doesn't lose that part of herself. She resists, but I've signed her up for a Russian math school and Russian acting classes, hoping she'll stay connected to her heritage.

Lastly, I've accepted that I can't go back to Moscow. It's tough, but I've found a way to make New York my new home. After immigrating, it's important to give yourself time to heal and process your emotions, including allowing yourself to cry. However, step by step, make an effort to learn about your new environment, even if you feel it's only temporary. Stay open to new experiences, don't take things too personally, and, most importantly, focus on learning the language and adapting to the habits of the people around you. Avoid surrounding yourself with familiar faces and environments. This is the time to step out of your comfort zone and embrace the learning process.

One of the main reasons I wrote this book boils down to the importance of staying the course. When you are about to leave your country or start something new, there will always be someone telling you why you shouldn't do it. They'll say you won't succeed, that no one will need you, and that no one will support you. Here's my response: Don't listen to them. These people more often than not wanted to make such a leap themselves but didn't have the strength or courage to do it. So they project their fears onto you. Yes, sometimes it feels like no one truly needs us, but in the end we owe it to ourselves to do what's best for us.

When I decided to leave Moscow, I heard I would never be as successful, that my lifestyle would never be the same, and most of all, that I was a fool to think I could achieve anything great in a place as competitive as New York. Sure, there were bumps along the way and I have to admit they were correct about some things: Sometimes it feels like no one truly needs me. I don't have a driver any more, but buses and Uber make my life convenient. I can't afford a big apartment, but my new home is very cozy. More importantly, three years after my new beginning, I can share that I've earned respectful reviews in national magazines, praise from well-known producers, and my kids have learned from my experience that you can lose everything and succeed again if you work hard. One day, someone told me that a runner is not the one who simply runs, but the one who decides one day that they are a runner and that they do their best at it every day. Same here — one day I decided that I would be a successful producer in New York and began working every day. I'm Sofia, an arts hustler, who found her way into the big American theater world. My experience may be unique, but it's also similar to others I have come to know. Some examples from the *Our Class* cast confirm that. Gus Birney dropped out of school to follow her own path while her classmates were grinding away to get into prestigious MFA programs. She is a star now. Andrey Burkovskiy was trained as a lawyer before becoming a famous actor in Moscow and later here in New York. Stephen Ochsner moved to Moscow, fell in love with the Russian language, but he had to abandon that life after the war and start again in New York. And of course, there's my Morris, who was born poor but through hard work and relentless pursuit of his dream, eventually made it to the top.

What I am trying to say is that your determination and commitment can carry you through even the toughest obstacles. I've also learned that people aren't simply good or bad, and there's rarely just one simple "right" way to do things. Like in *Our Class*, it's all about the circumstances we face and the choices we make in response. In one of the final scenes in *Our Class* Wladek chooses to tell the truth about the past, and another character confronts him asking, "Why are you saying these things? Which truth are you trying to tell? There are so many! Pick one! Pick the truth that will make you famous in your old age!" And in a strange way, I understand that. Life has taught me that people experience — and remember — things differently. Everyone holds their own version of the truth. But that doesn't mean we should stay silent out of fear and do nothing. If our intentions are honest and our purpose is clear, then we owe it to ourselves to keep going, and we'll always find a way to get where we want to be.

I had just finished writing the last chapter of this book when we received the notice from *The Wall Street Journal*, announcing that *Our Class* was included in its "Best Theater of 2024" list. That was a sign for me, as the universe whispered "You are back — like a horse on the track. Like a fish in the ocean." Right where I'm meant to be.

Our Class is moving forward, continuing its journey beyond New York, but it is now behind me. I've let it go in my mind. It feels like watching a child leave home, stepping into the world to find their own way. I am not sure if I will be working with Sara or Igor in the future, but I know that my journey as a hustler in performing arts will continue. Our team received so many awards, but honestly, winning an award doesn't matter to me anymore. I already feel like a winner. The Lucille Lortel golden statue, the most prestigious off-Broadway award, which I received as a producer for the best revival of a play, now sits on my bookshelf, beside books written by other immigrants who left Russia long before me. It's a symbol, recognition, yes — but the real reward is the quiet certainty I now carry: that I'm capable of building something from nothing. That I belong here. And that this is only the beginning.

I'm focusing on my next dream, and I know that, in the end, everything will be okay. If it's not okay, it's just not the end. But that's something for another chapter.

The End

www.ingramcontent.com/pod-product-compliance
Lightning Source LLC
Chambersburg PA
CBHW031510120626
46545CB00005B/1823